OUR PLANET:
How Much More Can Earth Take?

Are we using the Earth's resources wisely? Is our essential natural environment in danger? What do we have to do to secure our future on planet Earth? These are central issues of the "Sustainability Project." Renowned scientists have prepared twelve books with the objective of analyzing and explaining the most important aspects of and interrelations between the issues involved. Jill Jäger and her team of co-authors have contributed the introductory volume: *Our Planet: How Much More Can Earth Take?* The books in this series are putting the activities of mankind and the ongoing dynamic changes in the biosphere in perspective. They focus on various inter-relating aspects, such as the connection between resource and energy consumption, i.e. our production and consumer behavior, and the environmental liabilities thus created including climate change. Each book has a different focus and all of them together describe one system – Earth – from different perspectives. The respective contents of the books are systematically linked.

Jill Jäger is senior researcher at the Sustainable Europe Research Institute (SERI) in Vienna. Co-author of the books "Global Change and the Earth System: A Planet under Pressure" (Springer Verlag, 2004) and "Learning to Manage Global Environmental Risks" (MIT Press, 2001).

Our addresses on the Internet:
www.the-sustainability-project.com
www.forum-fuer-verantwortung.de
[English version available]

OUR PLANET:
How Much More Can Earth Take?

JILL JÄGER
In collaboration with Lisa Bohunovsky, Stefan Giljum, Fritz Hinterberger, Ines Omann and Doris Schnepf

Translated by Laura Radosh

Klaus Wiegandt, General Editor

HAUS PUBLISHING

First published in Great Britain in 2008 by
Haus Publishing Ltd
70 Cadogan Place
Draycott Avenue
London SW1X 9AH
www.hauspublishing.com

Originally published as: FORUM FÜR VERANTWORTUNG, *"Was verträgt unsere Erde noch"*, by Jill Jäger, in collaboration with Lisa Bohunovsky, Stefan Giljum, Fritz Hinterberger, Ines Omann and Doris Schnepf.
Ed. by Klaus Wiegandt
© 2007 Fischer Taschenbuch Verlag in der S. Fischer Verlag GmbH, Frankfurt am Main

English translation copyright © Laura Radosh 2008

The moral right of the author has been asserted

A CIP catalogue record for this book
is available from the British Library

ISBN 978-1-906598-05-1

Typeset in Sabon by MacGuru Ltd
Printed in Dubai by Oriental Press

CONDITIONS OF SALE

Mixed Sources
Product group from well-managed forests and other controlled sources
www.fsc.org Cert no. CU-COC-809367
© 1996 Forest Stewardship Council

FSC

Haus Publishing believes in the importance of a sustainable future for our planet. This book is printed on paper produced in accordance with the standards of sustainability set out and monitored by the FSC. The printer holds chain of custody.

Contents

Editor's Foreword

Sustainability Project

Sales of the German-language edition of this series have exceeded all expectations. The positive media response has been encouraging, too. Both of these positive responses demonstrate that the series addresses the right topics in a language that is easily understood by the general reader. The combination of thematic breadth and scientifically astute, yet generally accessible writing, is particularly important as I believe it to be a vital prerequisite for smoothing the way to a sustainable society by turning knowledge into action. After all, I am not a scientist myself; my background is in business.

A few months ago, shortly after the first volumes had been published, we received suggestions from neighboring countries in Europe recommending that an English-language edition would reach a far larger readership. Books dealing with global challenges, they said, require global action brought about by informed debate amongst as large an audience as possible. When delegates from India, China, and Pakistan voiced similar concerns at an international conference my mind was made up. Dedicated individuals such as Lester R. Brown and Jonathan Porritt deserve credit for bringing the concept of sustainability to the attention of the general public, I am convinced that this series can give the discourse about sustainability something new.

Two years have passed since I wrote the foreword to the initial German edition. During this time, unsustainable developments on our planet have come to our attention in ever more dramatic ways. The price of oil has nearly tripled; the value of industrial metals has risen exponentially and, quite unexpectedly, the costs of staple foods such as corn, rice, and wheat have reached all-time highs. Around the globe, people are increasingly concerned that the pressure caused by these drastic price increases will lead to serious destabilization in China, India, Indonesia, Vietnam, and Malaysia, the world's key developing regions.

The frequency and intensity of natural disasters brought on by global warming has continued to increase. Many regions of our Earth are experiencing prolonged droughts, with subsequent shortages of drinking water and the destruction of entire harvests. In other parts of the world, typhoons and hurricanes are causing massive flooding and inflicting immeasurable suffering.

The turbulence in the world's financial markets, triggered by the US sub-prime mortgage crisis, has only added to these woes. It has affected every country and made clear just how unscrupulous and sometimes irresponsible speculation has become in today's financial world. The expectation of exorbitant short-term rates of return on capital investments led to complex and obscure financial engineering. Coupled with a reckless willingness to take risks everyone involved seemingly lost track of the situation. How else can blue chip companies incur multi-billion dollar losses? If central banks had not come to the rescue with dramatic steps to back up their currencies, the world's economy would have collapsed. It was only in these circumstances that the use of public monies could be justified. It is therefore imperative to prevent a repeat of speculation with short-term capital on such a gigantic scale.

Taken together, these developments have at least significantly improved the readiness for a debate on sustainability. Many more are now aware that our wasteful use of natural resources and energy have serious consequences, and not only for future generations.

Two years ago, who would have dared to hope that WalMart, the world's largest retailer, would initiate a dialog about sustainability with its customers and promise to put the results into practice? Who would have considered it possible that CNN would start a series "Going Green"? Every day, more and more businesses worldwide announce that they are putting the topic of sustainability at the core of their strategic considerations. Let us use this momentum to try and make sure that these positive developments are not a flash in the pan, but a solid part of our necessary discourse within civic society.

However, we cannot achieve sustainable development through a multitude of individual adjustments. We are facing the challenge of critical fundamental questioning of our lifestyle and consumption and patterns of production. We must grapple with the complexity of the entire earth system in a forward-looking and precautionary manner, and not focus solely on topics such as energy and climate change.

The authors of these twelve books examine the consequences of our destructive interference in the Earth ecosystem from different perspectives. They point out that we still have plenty of opportunities to shape a sustainable future. If we want to achieve this, however, it is imperative that we use the information we have as a basis for systematic action, guided by the principles of sustainable development. If the step from knowledge to action is not only to be taken, but also to succeed, we need to offer comprehensive education to all, with the foundation in early childhood. The central issues of the future must be anchored firmly in school curricula, and no university student should be permitted to graduate without having completed a general course on sustainable development. Everyday opportunities for action must be made clear to us all – young and old. Only then can we begin to think critically about our lifestyles and make positive changes in the direction of sustainability. We need to show the business community the way to sustainable development via a responsible attitude to consumption, and become active within our sphere of influence as opinion leaders.

For this reason, my foundation *Forum für Verantwortung*, the ASKO EUROPA-FOUNDATION, and the European Academy Otzenhausen have joined forces to produce educational materials on the future of the Earth to accompany the twelve books developed at the renowned Wuppertal Institute for Climate, Environment and Energy. We are setting up an extensive program of seminars, and the initial results are very promising. The success of our initiative "Encouraging Sustainability," which has now been awarded the status of an official project of the UN Decade "Education for Sustainable Development," confirms the public's great interest in, and demand for, well-founded information.

I would like to thank the authors for their additional effort to update all their information and put the contents of their original volumes in a more global context. My special thanks goes to the translators, who submitted themselves to a strict timetable, and to Annette Maas for coordinating the Sustainability Project. I am grateful for the expert editorial advice of Amy Irvine and the Haus Publishing editorial team for not losing track of the "3600-page-work."

Taking Action — Out of Insight and Responsibility

"We were on our way to becoming gods, supreme beings who could create a second world, using the natural world only as building blocks for our new creation."

This warning by the psychoanalyst and social philosopher Erich Fromm is to be found in *To Have or to Be?* (1976). It aptly expresses the dilemma in which we find ourselves as a result of our scientific-technical orientation.

The original intention of submitting to nature in order to make use of it ("knowledge is power") evolved into subjugating nature in order to exploit it. We have left the earlier successful path with its many advances and are now on the wrong track, a path of danger with incalculable risks. The greatest danger stems from the unshakable faith of the overwhelming majority of politicians and business leaders in unlimited economic growth which, together with limitless technological innovation, is supposed to provide solutions to all the challenges of the present and the future.

For decades now, scientists have been warning of this collision course with nature. As early as 1983, the United Nations founded the World Commission on Environment and Development which published the Brundtland Report in 1987. Under the title *Our Common Future*, it presented a concept that could save mankind from catastrophe and help to find the way back to a responsible way of life, the concept of long-term environmentally sustainable use of resources. "Sustainability," as used in the Brundtland Report, means "development that meets the needs of the present without compromising the ability of future generations to meet their own needs."

Despite many efforts, this guiding principle for ecologically, economically, and socially sustainable action has unfortunately not yet become the reality it can, indeed must, become. I believe the reason for this is that civil societies have not yet been sufficiently informed and mobilized.

Forum für Verantwortung

Against this background, and in the light of ever more warnings and scientific results, I decided to take on a societal responsibility with my foundation. I would like to contribute to the expansion of public discourse about sustainable development which is absolutely essential. It is my desire to provide a large number of people with facts and contextual knowledge on the subject of sustainability, and to show alternative options for future action.

After all, the principle of "sustainable development" alone is insufficient to change current patterns of living and economic practices. It does provide some orientation, but it has to be negotiated in concrete terms within society and then implemented in patterns of behavior. A democratic society seriously seeking to reorient itself towards future viability must rely on critical, creative individuals capable of both discussion and action. For this reason, life-long learning, from childhood to old age, is a necessary precondition for realizing sustainable development. The practical implementation of the ecological, economic, and social goals of a sustainability strategy in economic policy requires people able to reflect, innovate and recognize potentials for structural change and learn to use them in the best interests of society.

It is not enough for individuals to be merely "concerned." On the contrary, it is necessary to understand the scientific background and interconnections in order to have access to them and be able to develop them in discussions that lead in the right direction. Only in this way can the ability to make appropriate judgments emerge, and this is a prerequisite for responsible action.

The essential condition for this is presentation of both the facts and the theories within whose framework possible courses of action are visible in a manner that is both appropriate to the subject matter and comprehensible. Then, people will be able to use them to guide their personal behavior.

In order to move towards this goal, I asked renowned scientists to present in a generally understandable way the state of research and the possible options on twelve important topics in the area of sustainable development in the series "*Forum für Verantwortung*." All those involved in this project are in agreement that there is no alternative to a united path of all societies towards sustainability:

- *Our Planet: How Much More Can Earth Take?* (Jill Jäger)
- *Our Threatened Oceans* (Stefan Rahmstorf and Katherine Richardson)
- *Water Resources: Efficient, Sustainable and Equitable Use* (Wolfgang Mauser)
- *Energy: The World's Race for Resources in the 21st Century* (Hermann-Joseph Wagner)
- *The Earth: Natural Resources and Human Intervention* (Friedrich Schmidt-Bleek)
- *Overcrowded World? Global Population and International Migration* (Rainer Münz and Albert F. Reiterer)
- *Feeding the Planet: Environmental Protection through Sustainable Agriculture* (Klaus Hahlbrock)
- *Costing the Earth? Perspectives of Sustainable Development* (Bernd Meyer)

- *The New Plagues: Pandemics and Poverty in a Globalized World* (Stefan Kaufmann)
- *Climate Change: The Point of No Return* (Mojib Latif)
- *The Demise of Diversity: Loss and Extinction* (Josef H Reichholf)
- *Building a New World Order: Sustainable Policies for the Future* (Harald Müller)

The public debate

What gives me the courage to carry out this project and the optimism that I will reach civil societies in this way, and possibly provide an impetus for change?

For one thing, I have observed that, because of the number and severity of natural disasters in recent years, people have become more sensitive concerning questions of how we treat the Earth. For another, there are scarcely any books on the market that cover in language comprehensible to civil society the broad spectrum of comprehensive sustainable development in an integrated manner.

When I began to structure my ideas and the prerequisites for a public discourse on sustainability in 2004, I could not foresee that by the time the first books of the series were published, the general public would have come to perceive at least climate change and energy as topics of great concern. I believe this occurred especially as a result of the following events:

First, the United States witnessed the devastation of New Orleans in August 2005 by Hurricane Katrina, and the anarchy following in the wake of this disaster.

Second, in 2006, Al Gore began his information campaign on

climate change and wastage of energy, culminating in his film *An Inconvenient Truth*, which has made an impression on a wide audience of all age groups around the world.

Third, the 700-page Stern Report, commissioned by the British government, published in 2007 by the former Chief Economist of the World Bank Nicholas Stern in collaboration with other economists, was a wake-up call for politicians and business leaders alike. This report makes clear how extensive the damage to the global economy will be if we continue with "business as usual" and do not take vigorous steps to halt climate change. At the same time, the report demonstrates that we could finance countermeasures for just one-tenth of the cost of the probable damage, and could limit average global warming to 2° C – if we only took action.

Fourth, the most recent IPCC report, published in early 2007, was met by especially intense media interest, and therefore also received considerable public attention. It laid bare as never before how serious the situation is, and called for drastic action against climate change.

Last, but not least, the exceptional commitment of a number of billionaires such as Bill Gates, Warren Buffett, George Soros, and Richard Branson as well as Bill Clinton's work to "save the world" is impressing people around the globe and deserves mention here.

An important task for the authors of our twelve-volume series was to provide appropriate steps towards sustainable development in their particular subject area. In this context, we must always be aware that successful transition to this type of economic, ecological, and social development on our planet cannot succeed immediately, but will require many decades. Today, there are still no sure formulae for the most successful long-term path. A large number of scientists and even more innovative entrepreneurs and managers will have to use their creativity and dynamism to solve the great challenges. Nonetheless, even today, we can discern the first clear goals we must reach in order to avert a looming catastrophe. And billions of consumers around the world can use their daily purchasing decisions to help both ease and significantly accelerate the economy's transition to sustainable development – provided the political framework is there. In addition, from a global perspective, billions of citizens have the opportunity to mark out the political "guide rails" in a democratic way via their parliaments.

The most important insight currently shared by the scientific, political, and economic communities is that our resource-intensive Western model of prosperity (enjoyed today by one billion people) cannot be extended to another five billion or, by 2050, at least eight billion people. That would go far beyond the biophysical capacity of the planet. This realization is not in dispute. At issue, however, are the consequences we need to draw from it.

If we want to avoid serious conflicts between nations, the industrialized countries must reduce their consumption of resources by more than the developing and threshold countries increase theirs. In the future, all countries must achieve the same level of consumption. Only then will we be able to create the necessary ecological room for maneuver in order to ensure an appropriate level of prosperity for developing and threshold countries.

To avoid a dramatic loss of prosperity in the West during this long-term process of adaptation, the transition from high to low resource use, that is, to an ecological market economy, must be set in motion quickly.

On the other hand, the threshold and developing countries must commit themselves to getting their population growth under control within the foreseeable future. The twenty-year

Programme of Action adopted by the United Nations International Conference on Population and Development in Cairo in 1994 must be implemented with stronger support from the industrialized nations.

If humankind does not succeed in drastically improving resource and energy efficiency and reducing population growth in a sustainable manner – we should remind ourselves of the United Nations forecast that population growth will come to a halt only at the end of this century, with a world population of eleven to twelve billion – then we run the real risk of developing eco-dictatorships. In the words of Ernst Ulrich von Weizsäcker: "States will be sorely tempted to ration limited resources, to micromanage economic activity, and in the interest of the environment to specify from above what citizens may or may not do. 'Quality-of-life' experts might define in an authoritarian way what kind of needs people are permitted to satisfy." (*Earth Politics*, 1989, in English translation: 1994).

It is time

It is time for us to take stock in a fundamental and critical way. We, the public, must decide what kind of future we want. Progress and quality of life is not dependent on year-by-year growth in per capita income alone, nor do we need inexorably growing amounts of goods to satisfy our needs. The short-term goals of our economy, such as maximizing profits and accumulating capital, are major obstacles to sustainable development. We should go back to a more decentralized economy and reduce world trade and the waste of energy associated with it in a targeted fashion. If resources and energy were to cost their "true" prices, the global process of rationalization and labor displacement will be reversed, because cost pressure will be shifted to the areas of materials and energy.

The path to sustainability requires enormous technological innovations. But not everything that is technologically possible has to be put into practice. We should not strive to place all areas of our lives under the dictates of the economic system. Making justice and fairness a reality for everyone is not only a moral and ethical imperative, but is also the most important means of securing world peace in the long term. For this reason, it is essential to place the political relationship between states and peoples on a new basis, a basis with which everyone can identify, not only the most powerful. Without common principles of global governance, sustainability cannot become a reality in any of the fields discussed in this series.

And finally, we must ask whether we humans have the right to reproduce to such an extent that we may reach a population of eleven to twelve billion by the end of this century, laying claim to every square centimeter of our Earth and restricting and destroying the habitats and way of life of all other species to an ever greater degree.

Our future is not predetermined. We ourselves shape it by our actions. We can continue as before, but if we do so, we will put ourselves in the biophysical straitjacket of nature, with possibly disastrous political implications, by the middle of this century. But we also have the opportunity to create a fairer and more viable future for ourselves and for future generations. This requires the commitment of everyone on our planet.

Klaus Wiegandt

Summer 2008

Authors' Foreword

In April 2005, Klaus Wiegandt traveled to Vienna to discuss his ambitious project "Forum for Responsibility" with Jill Jäger. He was looking for an author for the first book of his planned series; a book which was to explore the many aspects of global change and provide an introduction to the topic of sustainability.

Jill Jäger was pleased to accept the offer and accomplished this undertaking as part of her work at the Sustainable Europe Research Institute (SERI) in Vienna. SERI is a European network which researches sustainable development options for European societies. The institute examines the ecological, economic, social, and institutional conditions for sustainable development; analyzes and disseminates information on ecological limits; elucidates possible steps towards overcoming these ecological limitations; and creates scientifically accurate and practical policy proposals for sustainable development in Europe.

The book quickly became a project upon which six authors collaborated, bringing together the accumulated knowledge of SERI researchers versed in such topics as global change, resource use, work, the economy, and sustainable development.

Writing, and then discussing and commenting on each other's work brought us closer and made it even clearer to us how urgent and important the goal of sustainable development has become.

We would like to express our gratitude in particular to our

colleagues at SERI: Arno Behrens, Gabriela Christler, Mark Hammer, Sabine Maier, Anna Schreuer, and Andrea Stocker, as well as Jordis Grimm and Harald Hutterer. They read and criticized drafts and provided further support for our work on this book. Numerous friends and family members also helped us with their comments and ideas. We would also like to thank Professor Friedrich Schmidt-Bleek and Professor Bernd Meyer for their feedback on the manuscript, as well as Thomas Menzel for his incisive editing and Laura Radosh for the translation into English. Our particular thanks go to Klaus Wiegandt, who provided us with this opportunity to present our views.

Vienna, June 2008
Jill Jäger, Lisa Bohunovsky, Stefan Giljum,
Fritz Hinterberger, Ines Omann, and Doris Schnepf

Introduction

This book is the introductory volume to the series "Forum for Responsibility." It gives a description of our current situation on Earth and delineates possible actions we can take. When we discuss topics treated more comprehensively in other books of the series, we refer the reader to them.

Our main motivation for writing this book was the fact that the situation on our planet is much more dramatic than many people believe. However, we also wanted to show that there are things people can do. Instead of an extensive introduction, the following ten questions and answers delineate the issues we consider most important.

1 What kind of future do we want?

What will the world look like in fifty years? Will it be a world in which nature has no value and climate change causes catastrophes for people and economies every year? A world dominated by competition, in which the gulf between rich and poor is even greater than today? In other words, a fragmented world in which regions cut themselves off from or even fight one another? Or is there a chance it will be a peaceful world, in which the environment is protected and resources distributed fairly? If *it is* the peaceful world we want, we must begin to act today.

2 What does 'global change' mean?

The term "global change" is used in academic circles to describe the profound environmental changes that have been observed in the past years and decades: climate change, desertification, species extinction, etc. The causes of these changes can be found in the increasing number of people and their activities. Particularly disturbing is the fact that the pace at which our environment is being transformed increased dramatically in the second half of the 20th century (Chapter 1).

3 Is our situation really so dramatic, or do we still have time to act?

The situation is dramatic – for three reasons in particular: most of the main factors causing environmental change (such as economic growth, consumption in the industrialized countries, the size of the world population, consumption of resources and energy) continue to advance unchecked. The world population has been growing exponentially since the beginning of the last century. Meanwhile, the destruction of nature – the foundation of our existence – endangers the quality of life for the generations of today and tomorrow. Action is overdue (Chapter 1).

4 What are the driving forces behind environmental change?

Human activities are the main forces behind global change. Agriculture, food production, industry, the production of energy, urbanization, transportation, tourism, and international trade all have a bearing on the consumption of natural resources. These activities cause changes in the composition of the atmosphere, the characteristics of the Earth's surface, biodiversity, the global climate and the oceans' currents (Chapter 2).

5 Why do the industrialized countries need to reduce their resource consumption immediately?

The Earth can only withstand environmental burdens to a certain extent before our global ecosystems reach tipping points. It is the inhabitants of the rich industrialized countries who, due to their high level of consumption, are the main cause of environmental problems. They use up much more than they would be entitled to if resources were distributed fairly. Only if they reduce their resource consumption can people on other continents get their fair share of environmental space, and we can prevent the world from careering towards an ecological catastrophe. This demands fundamental changes in our economic systems and in our lifestyles. At the same time, population growth in developing countries must be slowed (Chapter 3).

6 Are technological innovations sufficient to reduce resource consumption?

In the past decades, we have observed similar developments in Europe and around the world: industries are using raw materials and resources more and more efficiently. One of the main reasons for this development is the utilization of new technologies. However, this has not relieved the world's ecosystems, because at the same time people are producing more and more goods and consuming more and more energy. Technological innovations alone are therefore an insufficient means of reducing resource consumption in the industrialized countries. Rather, additional measures are necessary which truly reflect the value of nature. These measures include prices that mirror real costs and a taxation system that supports "eco-efficient" products (Chapter 3).

7 Do we really need continuous economic growth to maintain our current standard of living?

Economic growth, alongside population growth, is one of the most important forces behind global environmental change. While people in the poor areas of the world need considerably more income in order to better their standard of living, more income makes fewer and fewer people in Europe, America, and Japan "happy." On the contrary: stress and isolation are increasing, consumption seems more and more like an addictive behavior, and illnesses caused by affluence (obesity, allergies) rather than shortages are on the rise. Individual well-being is increasingly found in "inner values" (contentment, relationships, communion with nature) and not in material affluence (Chapter 4).

8 What is sustainable development?

As early as 1987, more than twenty years ago, the World Commission on Environment and Development Report called for sustainable development (see Chapter 1 for a definition). Development that is sustainable prevents the destruction of the natural foundation of human existence and allows all people, today and in the future, to live happily and in peace without poverty or hunger. When development proceeds in a sustainable manner, there is a balance between poor and rich, between wasting resources and scarcity, and between the generations of today and those of tomorrow (Chapters 1 to 5).

9 Isn't it up to politicians to implement sustainable development?

At the Earth Summit of 1992 in Rio de Janeiro, the governments of the world made a commitment to sustainable development. In the Rio Declaration, for the first time ever, the right to sustainable development was established at global level. Unfortunately, in the years that followed, many of the promises made were not kept. This is also true of the Millennium Development Goals set by the United Nations in the year 2000.

International political targets are often not realized on the national level, because politics is dominated by short-term thinking and economic goals. Experience has shown that the general public, and the business community in particular, must participate in actions that support sustainable development. Only when politicians realize that they can win elections by fighting for sustainable development will they truly take the issue seriously (Chapter 5).

10 What can we do?

There are many political measures and instruments that can be used to increase resource productivity and decrease resource consumption. Both the environment and the economy can benefit from the right mix of instruments. Sustainable development necessitates rethinking on a societal level; this means setting new priorities, both on the part of society as a whole as well as of each and every individual. In our daily lives, we can all begin to make sustainability become a reality (Chapter 5).

1 Global Change

> "If I could sum it up in one sentence, I should say we are plundering our children's heritage to pay for our present unsustainable practices."
>
> Kofi Annan, Secretary General of the United Nations, presenting the Millennium Report, New York, 3 April 2000

Everyone is talking about "global change." In a nutshell, the term signifies the many transformations that our planet is undergoing at an increasing rate. In this chapter, we discuss the patterns and causes. In short, the changes are caused by the population explosion in the second half of the 20th century and by human economic activity, which has been steadily on the rise since the Industrial Revolution. Both developments have led to our planet changing at an ever-increasing speed. We provide a brief sketch of the most important changes in this context and their interconnectedness in the Earth system.

In recent decades, politics, science, and technology have been trying to meet the challenges of environmental change. Some steps have been made towards "sustainable development," but many have been taken only on paper. We want to take a closer look at this process and take stock: What have we achieved? Which goals have we yet to reach?

The Earth in its long history has undergone many vast transformations, for example continental drift and enormous climatic changes. Evolution also causes continuous change as species emerge and disappear.

For some years, however, it has become increasingly clear that it is human influences that are causing vast alterations in a very short time period. Floods, periods of drought, cyclones, air pollution, deforestation, desertification, water pollution; as well as globalization, growing poverty, epidemics, and the spread of information and communication technologies are all examples of developments that are part of global change. And they are happening faster and faster. One of the two main causes is population growth.

Population growth

Figure 1.1 illustrates some trends that demonstrate the connection between population growth and global change.

The global population (fig. 1.1a) was roughly half a billion people in the year 1700. This number increased only slowly over the next 200 years. Around 1900 however, it began to grow more quickly, and increased dramatically after 1950. The world's population rose from about 2.5 billion people to 6 billion by the end of the century. Whereas the population grew by approximately half a billion in the 200 years between 1700 and 1900, in the last fifty years of the 20th century, it increased by around four billion.

The Limits to Growth, published in 1972, made the exponential growth of the world's population clear. Exponential growth means that, in a defined period of time (for example one year), an increase is not by a constant amount, but by a constant factor in relation to the existing amount. Imagine a small pond with one (and only one!) water lily. This water lily begins to propagate,

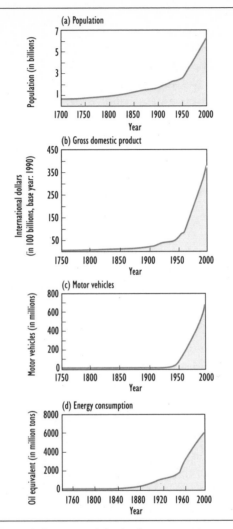

Figure I.I Changes in human activity in the past 300 years:
(a) world population; (b) global gross domestic product;
(c) motor vehicles; (d) energy consumption

so that its numbers double daily. If the plant were to continue to propagate unchecked, on the thirtieth day the pond would be completely covered, and all other living creatures in the pond would die. In the first days, however, the situation doesn't seem very dramatic. Nothing is done until the plants cover approximately half of the pond's surface. But this doesn't happen until the twenty-ninth day! Due to their exponential growth, the plants can cover the other half of the pond in only one day. Therefore, only one day remains to ward off the danger and save the pond.

Rainer Münz (who co-authored the book *Overcrowded World? Global Population and International Migration* in this series) estimates that the world's population is currently growing by 76 million people annually, or almost 210,000 per day. Is the pond named Earth, to use the image again, already half covered?

Population researchers at the UN expect the world's population to rise to about nine billion people by 2050, and perhaps even to 11–12 billion people by the year 2100. At the same time, during the 21st century, demographic aging will take place, and in some parts of the world we will observe population shrinking. Even if the rate of growth drops in the course of this century as compared to the second half of the 20th century, population growth will remain a problem in the future.

We must, however, also emphasize that the number of people alone is only part of the problem. Even when the birth rate in most industrialized countries falls, this does not necessarily mean that there is less pressure on the environment. One reason is that in place of traditional large families, there are many more singles. If more and more people own their own apartment or house, the amount of land consumed for living space increases, as does the consumption of resources.

There are many reasons – political, religious, and societal – why no resolute action has been taken against the problem

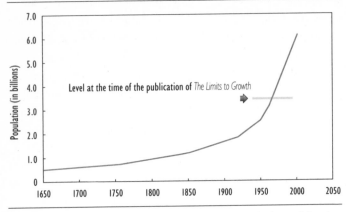

Figure 1.2 Growth of the world s population before and after publication of *The Limits to Growth*

of population growth. However, experts agree that the most important antidotes are primary education (alphabetization) and strengthening the role of women in society – particularly in developing countries.

Why is it so important to realize the goal of primary education for all? Even in 2005, more than 115 million children of elementary school age did not attend school. Most of them came from poor families in which the mother, too, often had no school education. Education, particularly for girls, helps all of society economically and socially. Educated women have more opportunities for economic independence and are more active in public life. They tend to have fewer and healthier children, who themselves attend school. Education is therefore the key to breaking the vicious cycle of poverty and population growth.

In five of the seven regions of the world, the goal of universal primary education has almost been achieved, but great efforts are still necessary in sub-Saharan Africa, South Asia, and Oceania. At the same time, it is necessary almost everywhere in the world to make sure that children complete their schooling and receive a comprehensive high-quality school education. In sub-Saharan Africa, for example, only a little less than half of all children finish elementary school. Children from poor families usually don't attend school at all, because they have to work.

Gender equality and strengthening the role of women is equally important. Equality between women and men is a human right, and is central to reducing population growth. Equality means equality in terms of education and work, and equal control over resources, as well as equal representation in public and political life. However, in South Asia, in Arab countries, and in sub-Saharan Africa, a much lower proportion of girls than boys are enrolled in school. According to the 2005 UN Report on the Millennium Development Goals, in sixty-five developing countries for which the necessary population data was completely available, 50% of the countries had achieved equality of boys and girls in primary education, and 20% of the countries in secondary education, but only 8% in higher education. Globally, women hold only 16% of parliamentary seats. Men dominate in decision-making processes in both politics and business. Finally, women, particularly in developing countries, also hold a much smaller proportion of paid positions of employment.

Klaus Hahlbrock's book in this series *Feeding the Planet: Environmental Protection through Sustainable Agriculture* also deals with the topic of population growth.

Economic activities

As we can see in Figure 1.1b, global gross domestic product barely rose between 1700 and 1900. Similar to the size of the population, growth began to accelerate after 1950. The global economy grew tenfold between 1950 and 2000. In the same period of time, the population increased threefold.

Many changes accompanied this growth of the global economy: for example, the number of motor vehicles (Fig. 1.1c) and global energy consumption (Fig. 1.1d). In these two areas as well, there was a considerable upsurge after 1950.

What are the consequences of escalating population size and human activity for our planet? The statistics portray an alarming picture, as Will Steffen and his co-authors have explained in detail.

Human activities have changed almost 50% of Earth's land surface, with drastic consequences for biodiversity, soil structure (and thus soil fertility), and our climate. Extinction of animal and plant species on land and in the water has risen dramatically, particularly since 1950. It is estimated that the current rate of extinction is one thousand times faster than it was in earlier geological periods.

Wetlands in coastal areas have been transformed by human activities and half of the mangrove forests have been destroyed.

Currently, more nitrogen is fixed by human activities than by natural processes. The production of chemical fertilizers, and in particular the emission of nitrogen oxide from combustion (power plants and motor vehicles) and from ammonia produced by intensive livestock farming, are changing Earth's so-called nitrogen cycle (Fig. 1.3a). This leads in turn to the eutrophication (over-fertilization) of soils and water bodies; our groundwater is polluted due to nitrate leaching from the soil. Furthermore, nitrogen oxides also contribute to acidification ("acid rain").

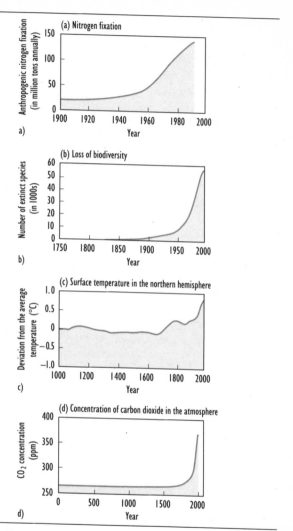

Figure 1.1 The effects of increased human activities: a) nitrogen fixation; b) animal and plant extinction; c) average temperature in the northern hemisphere; d) concentration of carbon dioxide in the atmosphere

The concentration of so-called greenhouse gases (such as carbon dioxide and methane) that contribute to global warming has increased considerably. Carbon dioxide is emitted into the atmosphere as the result of a variety of human activities, but in the main because of the combustion of fossil fuels (coal, crude oil, natural gas). The concentration of carbon dioxide in the atmosphere has not been at the level it is today for at least 650,000 years and has risen measurably since the Industrial Revolution (Fig. 1.3d). This has resulted in an increase in the average temperature of the Earth in comparison to the years 1000 and 1700 (Fig. 1.3c). Of the total rise in the Earth's temperature of 0.8°C observed in the past 100 years, around 0.6°C are the result of human activity. An additional, but smaller contribution to global warming of around 0.2°C is of natural origin. Should the concentration of greenhouse gases continue to rise sharply, we can expect more global warming than has ever been experienced by mankind by the year 2100 (see also Chapter 2). Changes in the concentration of greenhouse gases as a result of human activities are already causing unique alterations in our atmosphere's energy budget.

Global warming has led to a worldwide increase of extreme weather events in the past decades. It has also caused a decrease in the Earth's snow and ice cover. Warming oceans around the world and melting ice on land have already caused the sea level to rise by 10–20 centimeters. If greenhouse gas emissions continue to increase, so will extreme weather events, and the sea level will continue to rise.

In his book *Climate Change: The Point of No Return*, Mojib Latif describes the interconnectedness of the climate system and how human activities change our climate. He emphasizes the consensus among international climate researchers that human activities are influencing our climate to an ever greater degree.

Water plays an important role in many of the interconnections within the climate system. As Wolfram Mauser describes, solar energy drives the so-called hydrologic cycle, in which water evaporates, condenses, and precipitates and is then part of the run-off into rivers and groundwater. Compared to the total amount of water on Earth, only the tiny amount of 0.1% is active in the short-term hydrologic cycle relevant to humankind. The vast remainder of water on Earth is found in the large ocean basins and in ice, and moves only on a timescale of thousands of years. But this small percentage of water in the short-term hydrologic cycle distributes all usable water on Earth and makes it available to nature and humans.

However, more than half of all accessible fresh water resources are now being used for human purposes. Global reserves of fresh water are thus increasingly threatened by overuse as well as by pollution. Population growth, increasing human economic activity, and an improved quality of life are leading to an increase in rivalry for and conflicts about access to our limited fresh water resources. Water is an enormously valuable global natural resource; those regions that already suffer from water scarcity have a much greater awareness of its ecological and economic value than many societies in the industrialized countries.

Water in its liquid form is a precondition for the functioning and performance of our planet's life support system. To ensure this functioning, we have to expand our still limited knowledge of the resource water and the problems connected to it. Engineers, ecologists, and economists still all look at water from very different perspectives. The use of water and land, in the opinion of experts such as the above-mentioned Wolfram Mauser (who wrote the book in this series *Water Resources: Efficient, Sustainable and Equitable Use*), are two sides of the same coin, and yet an unbridgeable conflict of interest and lack of communication often seems to exist between agriculture and water management. As with other natural resources, the true value of the natural product water must be reflected in its price so that it is not wasted senselessly.

To use water effectively, we need to make technical progress. For example; we must breed plants that provide the same or better yields while using water more sparingly, we need to improve the efficiency of global irrigation systems and develop sources of animal protein that need less water to grow, or we must enlarge the usable portion of the Earth's surface. Today, aquacultures, for example, already produce a noticeable percentage of our protein needs. The development of simple and inexpensive water treatment plants to support water's natural self-cleaning ability, and increasing the efficiency of industrial water use are two of the tasks we need to tackle in the future.

For almost all people, the oceans are an entirely unknown environment. We are familiar only with a few coastal areas, a couple of fish species, and those pictures taken from orbit that reveal how large the oceans actually are. They cover no less than 70% of Earth's surface. Nevertheless, we know very little about what goes on in the depth of the seas. Katherine Richardson and Stefan Rahmstorf (*Our Threatened Oceans*) discuss the biological and physical characteristics of the oceans and show that they are a central element of the Earth system (see below and Chapter 2). They provide vivid examples of the connections between the components air, water, land, and life; of the existence of so-called thresholds (see below); and of the consequences of human activities.

One example for the interconnectedness of these components is that around half of the additional carbon dioxide released into the atmosphere due to human activity in recent years has been absorbed by the oceans. This affects the organisms that live in the oceans. Increasing carbon dioxide concentration on the ocean surface also makes it more acidic, lowering the pH. Due to this increased acidity, we can predict a negative impact for all organisms that produce calcium carbonate. Probably the most familiar producers of calcium carbonate are corals. Based on the expected pH and water temperature of the oceans, it has been calculated that almost all regions of the world's oceans that now boast conditions favorable to the production of calcium carbonate will disappear by the year 2065, if the concentration of carbon dioxide in the atmosphere continues to rise as projected by the Intergovernmental Panel for Climate Change (IPCC).

A further interconnectedness of components can be seen in the powerful ocean currents. The global pattern of ocean circulation is heavily affected by global warming. Due to climate-related changes of the North Atlantic Gulf Stream, global warming could possibly cause local areas – such as Europe – to cool down. In this case, thresholds in the system and interlinkages of chemical and physical processes play an important role.

Furthermore, human activities also have a decisive influence on the oceans' fish stocks. In the second half of the 20th century, there was a phenomenal increase in the exploitation of global fish stocks. Whereas in 1950, only around 5% of the oceans were completely exploited or even depleted by over-fishing; that figure is currently at approximately 80%. The consumption of edible fish has correspondingly increased fourfold in the past forty years. In the past century, fishing has depleted stocks of popular species in the world's oceans (such as tuna or cod) by 90%.

As Katherine Richardson elucidates, one of the main problems is the management strategy currently implemented most often by the fishing industry. This strategy assumes that there is a linear relationship between fish stocks and fishing pressure. When, for example, fishing grounds have been almost completely harvested, the assumption is that stocks will recover when fishing activity is suspended. Unfortunately, experience has shown that this is frequently not the case. Perhaps the best documented example is that of the cod stocks in Newfoundland. A moratorium went into effect here in 1992, but until today there has not been the slightest sign that stocks are recovering. No one can say which mechanisms prevent stocks from recovering, neither here, nor in other parts of the ocean. This development can certainly be seen as a component of global change. It confronts us with serious questions about the future of deep-sea fishing in the world's oceans and about the possible effects that over-fishing might have on the marine ecosystem.

Thresholds

At this point, we would like to emphasize the fact that none of these changes have a linear course of development. As we have already seen in Figures 1.1 and 1.2, many trends have accelerated in the past fifty years and, due to this process of acceleration, critical thresholds are being reached. When a threshold has been crossed, rapid changes take place, often unpredictably and dramatically. When tropical forests are clear-cut, this becomes particularly obvious. As long as only small areas are cleared, there is little influence on the number of animal and plant species. However, as soon as there is a certain degree of forest fragmentation, the rate at which biodiversity is lost accelerates significantly. This pattern – little or no changes up to a certain threshold, but as soon as it is crossed major changes that take place quickly – is a general rule in the Earth's natural system. A further problem is that in general, the threshold cannot be predicted. Therefore, we usually only know too late that a critical limit has been crossed.

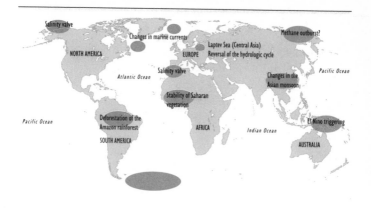

Figure I.4 Critical regions of the earth where crossing thresholds could have massive and unpredictable consequences

Hans-Joachim Schellnhuber from the Potsdam Institute for Climate Impact Research created a map highlighting critical elements in the Earth system (Fig. 1.4). When certain thresholds are crossed, the result is catastrophic changes. These include:

- the deforestation of the entire Amazon rainforest
- massive changes in marine circulation
- melting ice in Western Antarctica
- enormous changes in Asian monsoon patterns.

Clearly, such developments would have an enormous impact on humans, as environmental services (e.g. fresh water, food) would be severely restricted, and risks stemming from, for example, rising sea levels or climatic changes would increase dramatically.

Earth as a system

The examples of human-induced change described above are in themselves already impressive and cause for concern. However, merely listing them conceals the complexity of these changes and the fact that they are closely interconnected. One example is the growth of megacities. When we take a closer look, we can see that many of these cities are developing in coastal regions. This has a strong impact on the use of land, as well as on the oceans, and the atmosphere. At the same time, coastal regions are endangered by rising sea levels caused by global warming, and by the increasing intensity of extreme weather events (floods, droughts, tropical storms, etc.). In the cities, the gap between rich and poor is growing. Poor urban residents are less and less able to adapt to the consequences of environmental changes. This increases the likelihood of conflicts and reduces the quality of life in urban areas.

It is easy to extrapolate further chains of interdependencies. For example, human activities (particularly the combustion of fossil fuels) lead to a higher concentration of greenhouse gases in the atmosphere, which leads to climate change. This in turn causes a reduction of biological diversity and the further depletion of stratospheric ozone.

In a nutshell; physical, chemical, and biological processes on Earth are closely interconnected. Due to these connections, it is necessary to examine these processes holistically in order to understand all the impacts of human interference with natural processes. The idea of the Earth as a system emerged based on such insights (we shall return to this idea in Chapter 2). Katherine Richardson describes it as follows:

"A completely new discipline has developed recently, Earth

system science, the science of Earth as a system. This discipline attempts to understand how land, the atmosphere, and the oceans are interconnected, as well as the physical, chemical, and biological processes that take place in each component of the system, thereby influencing the course of events in other parts. The sum of all these interdependencies is the Earth system."

In the past few decades, science provided first insights into the complexity of the Earth system and showed how robust and at the same time how fragile it is. It is not possible to predict how the human activities described above will affect the Earth system. There are, however, some general statements we can safely make: human-induced changes in natural processes are as great as, or even greater than, those brought about by natural causes. They take place faster than changes caused by natural fluctuations, and have reached a pace and a scale, that have not been seen in the history of Earth in the past 500,000 years.

This is a just an outline of the current state of knowledge. When did scientists notice that something is wrong with the Earth system? What has been done to put a stop to these developments? In the following, we discuss some attempts that have been made to get a hold on those problems we now know about.

First scientific warnings

We have known how necessary it is to protect the environment for quite a long time. Since the beginning of the 20th century, all over the world national parks and other conservation areas have been founded. But not until the second half of the 20th century did environmental protection become a topic discussed by a broad public and taken up by international policy-makers.

The International Convention for the Regulation of Whaling (1946) and the Antarctic Treaty (1959) were the first international agreements on environmental issues. However, many see the publication of Rachel Carson's book *Silent Spring* in 1962 as the actual beginning of a broad public interest in environmental questions. For the first time, the book documented the many negative effects of the unchecked use of pesticides for agricultural purposes. Afraid that as a result of this, one day spring would come and no birds would sing, Carson wrote:

> "The resort to weapons such as insecticides to control [life] is a proof of insufficient knowledge and of an incapacity so to guide the processes of nature that brute force becomes unnecessary."

On the day of publication in late September 1962, 40,000 copies had already been ordered in advance. The book sparked off activity, affecting both governments and, at the time, scattered local environmental movements. The author did not, however, limit herself to only describing the problem. Particularly in the last chapter, she tried to point the way towards "the other road," as an alternative to conventional pest management, and described the long-term successes in fighting plant diseases and pests that had already been attained using natural enemies, insect illnesses, pheromone traps, and, most of all, cultivation suited to the area and crop rotation.

Ten years later, the growth of public interest in environmental questions was again attributed to a book. The above-mentioned report *The Limits to Growth* was the popularized summary of a large-scale Massachusetts Institute of Technology (MIT) study. Based on computer simulations, it showed that human society was soon going to reach its limits and collapse, if worldwide population growth, industrialization, food production, pollution, and resource consumption continued unchecked. However, the authors said, we were still in a position to modify our actions and change course.

Later, the authors were often criticized; because their predictions did not come to pass, their approach was obviously wrong. In reality, they had not calculated *prognoses* in their studies, but rather described *scenarios* that intentionally did not draw conclusions about the future. Going by the usual approach for scenarios "what will happen if," they wanted only to elucidate the basic tendencies of our growth-oriented economic system.

Due to the increasing interest in environmental protection, in June 1972 the first international UN conference on the topic of the environment was held in Stockholm. This conference is seen as the actual beginning of international environmental policy. More than 1,200 representatives from 112 countries (the former Eastern Bloc countries boycotted the conference) participated in the conference. June 5th, the first day of the conference, is still World Environment Day today.

The Declaration of the Stockholm Conference, developed by industrialized and developing countries, consists of twenty-six principles for environment and development accompanied by an action plan with 109 recommendations for actions to implement these principles. In the declaration, participating countries agree to transboundary cooperation in order to protect the environment.

First actions

The increasing interest in environmental questions and the first international environmental conference attended by government representatives led many countries to dedicate themselves to environmental policy for the first time. Ministries of the environment were founded and environmental programs developed. In the following decades, much was done to further the development of national and international environmental policy, whereby the first acts undertaken usually consisted of simple prohibitions or requirements, ignoring the interconnectedness of the Earth system. The impacts of human activities were thus mitigated, but the real causes of environmental changes were not always eliminated, as the following two examples clearly show.

Air pollution

Since the end of the 19th century, people have known that air pollution is an issue. Health problems were observed particularly near industrial plants and power plants. The first measures consisted of building higher smokestacks so that emissions would be carried away and diluted. However, in the late 1960s, regular water and soil quality measurements in Scandinavian countries showed that transboundary air pollution was responsible for overly high levels of acidity in lakes and soil. Higher smokestacks had lessened the problem of air pollution locally, but had caused problems in other places. The topic of air pollution was discussed at the 1972 Stockholm Conference for the first time – without concrete results. Not until 1979 was a convention negotiated which took up the problem.

In the Convention on Long-Range Transboundary Air Pollution, however, no goals were set for the reduction of emissions. This happened later in various agreements. The first protocols bound the countries which had ratified them to simple reduction goals for emissions of sulfur, and then for nitrogen oxides. Not until 1999 did thirty-one countries sign a protocol in Gothenburg,

Sweden setting emission reduction goals for sulfur, nitrogen oxides, ammonia, and volatile organic compounds; those pollutants mainly responsible for acidification and the formation of ground-level ozone. Threshold limits for the pollution of the soil (so-called critical loads) were also set. Furthermore, measures were agreed upon in order to reach these goals by the year 2010. The most important measure was setting ceilings for emissions from combustion plants (heating and industrial plants) and from the commercial use of organic solvents and motor vehicles. Furthermore, it called for the support of agricultural practices that contribute to a reduction of ammonia emissions from manure storage systems and spreading techniques, as well as from livestock husbandry.

International attempts to reduce transboundary air pollution were thus concentrated on Europe. Sulfur emissions have indeed been radically reduced – as has acid rain. However, international cooperation limited itself to reducing the emissions of power plants and motor vehicles. More basic questions, about lifestyle, for example, or the true need for mobility, were not discussed.

The depletion of stratospheric ozone

Ozone is made up of three oxygen atoms (O_3). In Earth's atmosphere, 90% of all ozone is in the stratosphere, the layer which is between ten and fifty kilometers above the earth (10% is mostly in the lower atmosphere). In the stratosphere, ozone molecules are constantly broken down and combined again. Without ozone in the stratosphere, life on earth as we know it would not be possible, because ozone absorbs the biologically harmful ultraviolet radiation emitted by the sun. In humans, ultraviolet radiation can cause skin cancer.

Hans-Jochen Luhmann's book *Die Entdeckung der Bedro-hung der Ozonschicht – ein Hindernislauf oder Wir sind noch einmal davongekommen* (*The Discovery of the Threat to the Ozone Layer – An Obstacle Course or Yet Another Close Call*) tells the story of how the danger of ozone depletion in the strato-sphere was discovered just in time. Two scientists in the USA discovered in 1974 that human activity can destroy the ozone layer. Sherwood Rowland and Mario Molina showed that chlo-rofluorocarbons (CFCs), used for example in aerosol sprays, do not cause any chemical reaction in the lower strata of the Earth's atmosphere, but are transported to the stratosphere above. There, the high-energy ultraviolet light of the sun breaks down the CFC molecules. The result is chlorine radicals, freed after the CFC compounds are broken down in the stratosphere, which go on to break down ozone molecules.

In the eleven years after this discovery was made, some coun-tries banned the use of CFCs in aerosol sprays, but there was no worldwide ban. In 1985, the International Convention for the Protection of the Ozone Layer was signed, but it contained no commitments. Rather, it was a framework for further negotia-tions. The problem had been recognized, but no measures were taken to solve it.

In 1985, the hole in the ozone layer over Antarctica was dis-covered. Joe Farman, a British scientist, published a time series of measurements of ozone in the stratosphere above Antarctica. Farman had first noticed the depletion of ozone in the Antarctic spring of 1982, but he delayed publication of the data, because he did not trust his observations. After all, satellite measure-ments had to date not found any signs of a dramatic depletion of the ozone layer over Antarctica. The publication of Farman's measurements in 1985 got the ball rolling. The satellite data were reevaluated, and it confirmed the reduction in ozone over the South Pole in the spring. Thus, measurements both from the ground and from satellites showed that the ozone in the stratosphere above Antarctica was greatly reduced in spring.

The hole in the ozone layer was there, but how could it be explained? How was it connected to CFC emissions? What were the chemical processes involved, and what role did meteorology play? It was to take a bit more than two years until scientists could satisfactorily explain the depletion of ozone. In the end, this explanation then mirrored the complexity of the Earth system in its entirety. Chemistry, physics, meteorology, the long polar nights at the South Pole – they all were part of the explanation.

In September 1987 in Montreal, significant measures to protect the ozone layer were finally made obligatory. The Montreal Protocol was written in a fashion that allowed controls to be tightened regularly. First, ceilings were set for the emissions of ozone-depleting chemicals, then they were completely banned – a successful strategy: there has been a decrease in ozone layer depletion, but it will take many decades until it has regained its "normal" value. Admittedly, some countries still do not fulfill their obligations, and CFCs are still sold through the channels of organized crime.

Yet another close call, as Luhmann remarked quite rightly. But the topic of the hole in the ozone layer once again confirms that the Earth is a very complex system. CFC emissions came mostly from the northern industrialized countries, but the hole developed at the South Pole. The gases were emitted at the Earth's surface, but the impact was on the higher atmospheric strata. Paul Crutzen, who won the Nobel Prize in Chemistry together with Sherwood Rowland and Mario Molina for his work on stratospheric ozone, sees parallels to the topic of global warming:

"The ozone hole is the result of a chemical instability in the atmosphere caused by human activities. It appeared in the area furthest away from the origin of the emission of CFC gases. No atmospheric scientist foresaw its appearance and its complex behavior. This proves that humans are capable even of considerable destruction to their global environment, and that our ability to predict the consequences of human activities is limited. This puts even greater demands on our duty to exercise precaution. I refer in particular to the problem of global warming."

The depletion of ozone in the stratosphere is a good example of a non-linear coupled system, and it shows how human activities can cause instabilities. The speed at which the ozone hole developed confirms the important role played by thresholds: when the concentration of certain chemicals in the stratosphere reached critical mass, abrupt changes took place.

Paul Crutzen also points out that we were very lucky to have avoided a greater catastrophe. Had the chemical industry used bromine rather than chlorine, the effects would have been much more serious. Bromine functions much like chlorine in coolants and insulants, but one atom of bromine is 100 times more effective than chlorine in breaking down ozone. Had bromine been used, Crutzen says, we would have been faced – with no warning – with a global ozone-layer hole year-round already in the 1970s, and not only a hole in the ozone layer over Antarctica in the spring. Even worse, scientists of the period would have been unable to identify the problem and make the necessary measurements.

The American political scientist Edward Parson conducted a thorough analysis of the history of the ozone hole and the negotiations on the protection of the ozone layer. He concluded that the 1987 Montreal Protocol is an example of a political negotiation strategy that could be applied to other problems as well. Science and technology were successfully integrated into the negotiations.

The fact is, with the support of almost all nations and of business and industry as well, global consumption of ozone-depleting chemicals was reduced by 95%. However, this was not achieved by the original reduction goals, but rather by measures that became increasingly stringent, while at the same time many (technical) innovations were made that reduced chemical consumption – a development that could easily serve as a model for climate policy.

The call for sustainable development

When we interfere with natural processes, we are confronted with ever greater challenges. Not only the complex and interconnected changes in the Earth system described above, but also and at the same time similarly complex changes in many social and economic factors. If we do not want to further harm our planet without being able to gauge the consequences, we need new concepts that can better integrate economic development with the complexity of the Earth.

One of these concepts is provided by the term "sustainable development," which approaches environment and development together. The term was first given broad attention in the World Commission on Environment and Development's so-called Brundtland Report, entitled *Our Common Future*. The Commission was established by the United Nations in 1983. It was the third Commission after the Brandt Commission on North-South relations and the Palme Commission on security issues. The United Nations General Assembly founded the Commission due to much dissatisfaction in the international community over the inability to get global problems under control. Its task was to generate a report on the perspective for environmentally-friendly development that could function in the long term and at the global level until the year 2000 and beyond. The Commission was composed of nineteen members from eighteen countries around the world. The then Prime Minister of Norway, Gro Harlem Brundtland, previously Minister of the Environment, was elected as Chair. In 1987, the Commission's final report was published, and it was to have a decisive influence on the international deliberations on developmental and environmental policy. In a much cited sentence, the Commission demands development "that meets the needs of the present without compromising the ability of future generations to meet their own needs."

Until today, this remains the globally accepted definition of "sustainable development." The Commission furthermore came to the conclusion that sustainable development can be achieved only by integrating it into all political sectors. Problems usually considered separately, such as pollution in industrialized countries, the global arms race, the debt crisis, population growth, and desertification in the Third World must be seen as interlinked. Individual measures that do not take this interconnectedness into account will not help solve these problems.

The Commission believed that different goals for sustainable development were appropriate for industrialized and developing countries. Developing countries must eradicate poverty. In the industrialized countries, on the other hand, material affluence must be made to harmonize with the conservation of nature as the foundation of our existence. It is clear in this context that the consumerism and lifestyle of people in the industrialized countries cannot be a model for the current and future population of the entire world.

While the global economy must satisfy the needs and legitimate desires of humankind, the Commission warned that unchecked economic growth could exceed the ecological limits of the Earth. This also means that people must change many of their activities and their lifestyles if the world is not to be confronted with unacceptable human suffering and environmental damage. The Commission called for "a new era of economic growth – growth that is forceful and at the same time socially and environmentally sustainable."

The UN Conference on Environment and Development in Rio de Janeiro

Five years after the Brundtland Report was published, and twenty years after the first International Conference on the Environment in Stockholm, the UN Conference on Environment and Development convened in Rio de Janeiro (see http://www.un.org/geninfo/bp/enviro.html). Its only purpose was to further develop the Brundtland Commission's recommendations for reaching the goal of sustainable development, and create a politically and legally binding plan of action. Both development and environmental issues were to be addressed. Around 10,000 delegates from 172 countries participated. The conference, commonly known as the Earth Summit, set new standards for the participation of civil society organizations in international processes. Altogether, 2,400 representatives of non-governmental organizations (NGOs) participated in the conference; the NGO Forum, which took place at the same time, was attended by a further 17,000 people. It was a long journey from the opening of the conference until delegates were able to pass important resolutions, a journey during which participating governments grappled with each other fiercely at times. In the end, five documents were signed:

- The Rio Declaration on Environment and Development
- The United Nations Framework Convention on Climate Change
- The United Nations Convention on Biological Diversity
- The Statement of Forest Principles
- Agenda 21.

The Rio Declaration on Environment and Development refers directly to the Brundtland Commission's recommendations and emphasizes the fact that economic progress is possible only in combination with environmental protection. To achieve this, countries must form new and equal partnerships worldwide with the participation of governments, the people, and key elements of society. For the first time in history, the twenty-seven principles of the Rio Declaration established a global right to sustainable development. The precautionary principle and the polluter pays principle were also recognized as guiding principles. The Rio Declaration also mentions the most important preconditions for sustainable development:

- The eradication of poverty
- Appropriate demographic policy
- Reduction and elimination of unsustainable consumption and production patterns
- Comprehensive public participation in decision-making processes.

The rights of present and future generations are incorporated in the Rio Declaration. It also demands an end to the discrimination of disadvantaged groups such as women, youth and indigenous peoples.

The UN Framework Convention on Climate Change

(UNFCCC) was negotiated before the conference in Rio and signed at the Earth Summit. The objective of the Convention is to achieve stabilization of greenhouse gas concentrations (carbon dioxide, methane, and four other gasses) in the atmosphere at a level low enough to prevent dangerous interference with the global climate system. The convention requires signatory states to establish national greenhouse gas inventories (regular accounts of emissions from various sources), and to develop programs to reduce emissions. Five years later, the Kyoto Protocol was signed, which sets concrete emission reduction goals. The Protocol is a first step towards achieving the objective of the UNFCCC.

The Convention on Biological Diversity (CBD) has as its goals the preservation of biological diversity and the sustainable use of biological resources. Animal and plant species are to be protected, endangered ecosystems and the genetic resources within them must be safeguarded. Signatory states are to create legislation for the protection of species threatened by extinction, establish protected natural areas, aid the recovery of damaged ecosystems, and support the protection of endangered species. Signatories are also bound to facilitate access to genetic resources within their borders for the purpose of sustainable use. There were intense and controversial discussions on this last topic; between industrialized countries and developing countries, for example, on the economic advantages gained by patenting genetic material from tropical rainforests.

The Statement of Forest Principles is concerned with the ecological management, conservation, and sustainable development of the world's forests. It is a non-binding declaration of intent. Participants could not agree upon the binding forest convention demanded by the industrialized countries over the objections of developing countries that did not want to lose their sovereignty over their natural resources. The statement of intent includes the following:

– All countries should participate in "greening the world" by means of reforestation and forest conservation.
– Each country should implement a national forest policy based on the principle of environmental compatibility. This includes the ecological management of areas adjacent to forests.
– Trade in forest products is to be based on non-discriminatory rules agreed upon multilaterally. International trade in timber and other forest products must not be banned or restricted by unilateral measures.
– Possible causes of pollution, for example "acid rain," must be carefully monitored and controlled.

After the Rio Summit, the Statement of Forest Principles was made more concrete in further negotiations. The economic interests of the developing countries were given greater attention.

Finally, *Agenda 21* consists of forty chapters containing detailed measures meant to ensure the implementation of sustainable development. The chapters are divided into four sections:

– Social and economic dimension: Poverty alleviation, population and demographic dynamics, promoting health and promoting sustainable settlement patterns;
– Conservation and management of resources for development: climate protection, combating deforestation, preservation of biological diversity, and environmentally-friendly waste disposal;
– Strengthening the role of major groups: Participation of diverse social players (the so-called major groups are:

women, children and youth, indigenous peoples, NGOs, workers and trade unions, industry and business, science and technology, farmers) of utmost importance to the implementation of the Agenda;

– Means of implementation: General conditions necessary for implementation, such as technology transfer, education, and international cooperation.

The Earth Summit thus functioned as an implementation committee for the Brundtland Commission, with participants from around the globe laying the foundation for sustainable development. Environmental and development policy were coupled with detailed implementation measures. Of course, as in all political processes, compromises were made, but the majority of the Brundtland Commission's recommendations were followed.

The Millennium Development Goals

In the year 2000, the Millennium Development Goals (MDG) were agreed upon at the United Nations' Millennium Summit in New York. Targets to be achieved by the year 2015 were set in order to reach the MDGs. The goals themselves were later also integrated into the Johannesburg Conference's Plan of Implementation (see below).

Goal 1: Eradicate extreme poverty and hunger. Halve the number of people whose income is less than one US dollar a day. Halve the proportion of people suffering from hunger.

Goal 2: Achieve universal primary education. All boys and girls should be able to complete a full course of basic education.

Goal 3: Promote gender equality and empower women. Eliminate gender disparity in primary and secondary education preferably by 2005, and at all levels of education by 2015.

Goal 4: Reduce child mortality. Reduce the mortality rate of children under five by two-thirds.

Goal 5: Improve maternal health. Reduce the maternal mortality rate by three-quarters.

Goal 6: Combat HIV/AIDS, malaria, and other diseases. The spread of HIV/AIDS should be halted and the virus forced to retreat. Prevent outbreaks of malaria and other major diseases.

Goal 7: Ensure environmental sustainability. The principles of sustainable development should be integrated into national policy; the loss of resources should be reversed. Halve the proportion of people without sustainable access to safe drinking water. Furthermore, achieve significant improvement in the lives of at least 100 million slum-dwellers by 2020.

Goal 8: Develop a global partnership for development. Develop further an open trading and financial system that is rule-based, predictable, and non-discriminatory. Address the special needs of the least developed countries in an appropriate manner. Deal comprehensively with the debt problems of developing countries with low and middle incomes through national and international measures in order to make debt bearable in the long term.

The Johannesburg Summit 2002

Ten years after the Rio Summit, the next UN conference on sustainable development convened in Johannesburg; the *World Summit on Sustainable Development* (WSSD). This time, approximately 20,000 representatives of governments, business, and non-governmental organizations participated. Again there were many ambitious plans, including the evaluation of the implementation of Agenda 21 and of national action plans for sustainability, and setting new objectives and measures for sustainable development.

The summit found that little had been achieved in the implementation of Agenda 21 as well as of national action plans. On the other hand, there were also reports on some successful initiatives. The political negotiations were long and drawn-out. The World Summit ended with an official statement by the heads of state and government (The Johannesburg Declaration on Sustainable Development) and the Johannesburg Plan of Implementation which details the Millennium Development Goals and the measures that need to be taken to ensure sustainable development.

What has been achieved?

The basic idea of sustainable development was born and defined more than twenty years ago, and presented to the global public in 1987. Since then, as described above, there have been many discussions at international conferences, and many agreements have been made. Furthermore, national and international "sustainability strategies" have been developed, and partially also implemented, but the objectives have not been achieved at all – on the contrary.

Poverty continues to grow

Today, there are still one billion people who must get by on less than one dollar a day. There have been some regional improvements: for example, the number of people living on less than one dollar a day in Asia fell by almost a quarter of a billion between 1990 and 2001. However, this is due mostly to economic growth in China and India. Developments in China are the main reason for success in the global struggle against poverty in the past twenty years. On the other hand, statistics show that overall poor people are becoming even poorer. The average income of the extremely poor people in sub-Saharan Africa decreased between 1990 and 2001. Between 1981 and 2001, the number of people in sub-Saharan Africa forced to get by on less than one dollar a day doubled from 164 million to 313 million. In Latin America and the Caribbean, the number rose from 36 to 50 million. The proportion of people in Eastern Europe and Central Asia forced to live on less than two dollars a day rose from 2% in 1981 to 20% in 2001, according to data published by the World Resources Institute in 2005.

This negative record is confirmed by the 2005 *Human Development Report*, the annual report of the United Nations Development Program (UNDP). Five years after the Millennium Development Goal targets were set, there was indeed some progress in the fight against poverty. For example, a global campaign in 2005 was successful regarding development aid and a debt relief deal agreed upon at the G8 Summit. But the big picture is sobering. According to the UNDP, targets will not be met in many countries. The truth is, as the UNDP has pointed out, that the promises made to the world's poor have not been kept.

In industrialized countries as well, poor people are becoming increasingly poorer. In the USA for example, the number of poor people increased steadily between 2000 and 2005. In 2006, the poverty rate for minors in the United States was 21.9% – the highest child poverty rate in the developed world.

Resource consumption still increasing

The industrialized countries' goal to bring material affluence into harmony with the conservation of nature, the foundation of our existence, has not been achieved. Material affluence continues to grow in the industrialized countries; the conservation of nature remains in jeopardy. Although some environmental problems have been at least partially solved (see the account of the problems of air pollution and the depletion of stratospheric ozone in this chapter), globalization has led to the transfer of the industrialized countries' material and energy intensive patterns of consumption and lifestyles to poorer countries – a disastrous development. Developing countries are right in demanding an improvement in their standard of living. However, the industrialized countries must help find ways to reach this goal sustainably and at the same time harmonize their own standard of living with nature. Instead, ever more threshold countries are copying non-sustainable industrialized country lifestyles.

Norman Myers and Jennifer Kent carried out a comprehensive study of the phenomenon of the 'new consumers.' The countries with an average economic growth of 5% annually over the past ten years and a population of at least twenty million are:

– in Asia: China, India, South Korea, the Philippines,
   Indonesia, Malaysia, Thailand, Pakistan;
– in the Middle East: Iran, Saudi Arabia;
– in Africa: South Africa;

- in Latin America: Brazil, Argentina, Venezuela, Colombia, Mexico;
- in Eastern Europe: Turkey, Poland, the Ukraine, Russia.

China, with a total population of almost 1.3 billion and an economic growth rate of over 10% annually, boasts 300 million "new consumers." The situation is similar in India, where 130 million inhabitants enjoy growing affluence. Two-fifths of the new consumers in the twenty countries listed above come from these two countries alone.

In all of these countries, increasing economic affluence has also led to an increase in the consumption of energy, material, and land area – to different extents, but the tendency is clear (see the 2005 report "Fair Future" by the Wuppertal Institute).

In terms of absolute energy consumption, the industrialized countries are still ahead, but the new consumers are quickly catching up. Consumption patterns are also changing. New consumers have a large proportion of meat in their diets, and they own cars and many other consumer goods. For example, since the beginning of the 1990s, more television sets can be found in the new consumer countries than in the developed industrialized countries.

Summary

For at least the past twenty years, it has been clear that we have to bring economic and social development in tune with natural processes. Since then, "sustainable development" has become an international, national, and regional goal. But despite gigantic world summits, despite promising declarations and strategies, the finish line is still far in the distance. The processes described above make it clear that international and national policy-makers' ability to provide solutions is limited. The main obstacle is that political and economic policy is usually set for short-term goals – less than five years – whereas sustainable development is a long-term goal that can be realized only by implementing the appropriate short-term objectives step by step. That's why some voices can even be heard saying that we are farther away from sustainability than we were twenty years ago. And in fact, the list of missed objectives is long. Let us take one more look at the *status quo*:

- The knowledge we have of our situation is ignored in political and business circles. The long-term goal of "sustainable development" is disregarded in favor of short-term profit.
- Population growth is still a taboo topic.
- Since the Earth Summit in 1992, the rich countries have failed to keep their promises.
- The number of people living in absolute poverty continues to grow.
- Industrialized country consumption continues to grow.
- Development aid is still insufficient and is burdened by too many constraints.
- Prices still do not reflect the value of nature.
- Military conflicts still cause human tragedies and immense environmental damage.
- Overfishing, pollution, and unchecked growth in coastal areas endanger our oceans.
- Pressure on our scarce fresh water resources is mounting.
- AIDS wreaks havoc in developing countries, particularly in Africa.
- Despite the Biodiversity Convention, thousands of species become extinct each year.

At least this list of targets not met is complemented by some successes:

- An international agreement (the Montreal Protocol) slowed the destruction of the stratospheric ozone layer.
- Although there has hardly been any progress at the policy-making level, thousands of small practical projects that support sustainable development have sprung up at local level.
- Civil society is increasingly involved in political processes.
- Business and industry is increasingly recognizing its responsibility (keyword: "corporate social responsibility").
- More people have better access to information.
- Scientists have made major advances in helping us better understand the complexity of the Earth system.
- Accurate indicators and improved monitoring give us a realistic picture of just how far we are from reaching the goal of sustainability.
- With the Kyoto Protocol, first steps towards solving the problem of global warming have been taken.
- Many countries have implemented strategies towards sustainable development.
- Further environmental agreements have been negotiated.

These lists of successes and failures were compiled by the International Institute for Sustainable Development (see http://www.iisd.org/briefcase/ten+ten_contents.asp). What does this juxtaposition show us? Can we reach the goal of sustainable development? The answer – that we support in later chapters of this book – is a clear "yes!" We cannot afford to wait until the effects of global warming and the pollution of our air and water reach catastrophic dimensions – and hope that we can adapt somehow. Rather, we must build on the successes that we have achieved and continue to work towards the goal of sustainability.

2 The Earth System

The Earth is a complex system consisting of many closely inter-connected subsystems. As we have described in the first chapter, this means that human interference has diverse, often unpredicted or undesired, impacts. If everything on our planet functioned according to the simple principle of cause and effect, it would be possible to solve environmental, economic, or social problems simply by intervening at the right point. In reality however, there is usually not just *one* point – and when you think you've found it, it often does something completely different, or there are other unwanted side effects that accompany the intended effect.

Therefore, if we want to prevent negative developments, whether ecological, economic, or social, we must understand the Earth system as a whole and make allowances for its intercon-nected nature. In this chapter, we therefore take a closer look at the Earth system touched upon in Chapter 1. We explain why simple cause and effect relationships rarely exist and, using three examples of human-induced changes, illustrate complex chains of relationships.

What is a system?

A system consists of a (larger) number of elements and their characteristics as well as the relationships between these elements and interactions with the surrounding environment. The environment of the Earth system is outer space. The environment of a pond system is the surrounding fields and farmland. A system is a whole and as such can be delimited from its surroundings. The relationships between its elements manifest themselves by the exchange of material, energy, or information and are decisive for the structure of the system.

Complex systems are usually made up of many smaller systems – as is the Earth. These subsystems can be roughly divided into two groups: *natural systems* and *socio-economic* systems. Some examples of natural systems are: oceans, forests, deserts, ponds, or even atoms. Socio-economic systems are systems founded by people, such as economic or political systems, businesses, cities, regions, or the European Union. The individual subsystems of Earth are connected to one another; this means they trade material, energy, or information and they have a reciprocal influence upon each other's development.

Natural systems are the basis of all forms of life and development. We refer to them here as "nature" or – from a human point of view – as "the environment." In socio-economic systems, people (inter)act. These systems have artificial boundaries and are also defined by humans. Their structures, rules, and laws are set up by people as well. Socio-economic systems are able to learn; they can set and also change goals when adapting to new conditions within the above-mentioned structures and rules. The individuals in socio-economic systems – the people, that is – think about their behavior, relate with others, and reflect on their actions and the consequences of their actions. They are also able to turn a crisis into a learning opportunity and become better able to cope with similar situations in the future.

Many of the systems in which we are interested are mixed systems. They contain subsystems from both groups (natural and socio-economic) that can overlap and interact with one another. For example, the forest, a natural system, is part of a region, which is a socio-economic system. The inhabitants of this region use the forest for rest and recreation as well as for economic purposes (wood, hunting, mushrooms). By absorbing carbon dioxide, the forest also contributes to the maintenance of the carbon cycle and to better air quality. The region's inhabitants care for the forest, plant new trees, and use it for leisure. Forest and humans have a reciprocal influence on, and are dependent upon, one another. If people stop working in the forest, it can no longer exist in the same form. When the human socio-economic system changes and with it activities in the forest, the forest also changes. If the forest changes, for example because of global warming, humans must adapt.

The Earth consists of subsystems on a variety of spatial levels. Human cells, molecules, and atoms are subsystems, as are the atmosphere and the biosphere. Subsystems on higher levels themselves contain subsystems on lower levels. In this manner, hierarchies are formed. Thus a traffic system is part of a city, a person is part of a family, and a frog is part of a pond. There are many connections between these levels, as well as between subsystems on the same level, for example between two regions. There are also connections between natural and socio-economic systems; for example, between a river and the city it flows through.

Subsystems of the Earth system are themselves systems made up of many components, or of further subsystems. The systems we examine here, whether the Earth itself, whether natural or socio-economic, are characterized by their complexity. They are contrasted by simple systems.

Simple systems

Simple systems can be described precisely. Their development is predictable and can be calculated, and they display clear cause and effect relationships. Simple systems are often closed systems, isolated from their surroundings. They are usually static and man-made. An example of a static system is a library catalog system.

Complex systems

Complex systems are distinguished by a series of characteristics, some of which are described below. The boundary between a simple system and a complex system is not always easy to delineate. Not every complex system exhibits all of the characteristics described below. Depending on the system, some characteristics will be more or less developed. Degrees of complexity vary. In general, the more variation there is between individual elements and the more relationships there are between the elements, the more complex a system is. A close look at these characteristics quickly shows why these systems are called "complex:"

– Openness: The system is open to its surroundings and to other systems; it is in contact with its environment. It is influenced from outside and also affects its surroundings through the flow of information, material, etc. into and out of the system. Outflows are often reactions to inflows. They are the system's manner of responding to external challenges. All living systems are open. The Earth itself is an open system, exposed to outer space with which it exchanges material and energy (e.g. comets and solar radiation).

- Dynamics: The system is never in a stable equilibrium for long, but is in a process of constant change. "You never step into the same river twice," as the Greek philosopher Heraclitus declared 2,500 years ago. The river is in constant flux and will never again be exactly the same as it was. One form of change is growth, which can take place in different ways. Using the forest as an example once more: a forest is constantly absorbing external materials and emitting them again; it absorbs solar energy and also emits energy in the form of heat or stored energy (wood, plants). In this way, the forest changes constantly; new trees grow, others fall over; new pollen and seeds are brought in, etc.

- Close, usually non-linear, interactions between the elements: An input into the system does not always cause a proportional output. Rather, the output can be stronger or weaker. Small causes can have very large effects. Conversely, a large input may have very little impact. One example is the Australian rabbit plague. To please some hunters in Australia, a limited number of rabbits were released; within a short period of time, the country faced a massive rabbit plague. The animals, imported from Europe, had no natural enemies in Australia, and therefore the population exploded. Reciprocity can thus be either positive (strengthening) or negative (weakening), faint or formidable, and it can change directions over the course of time. In a complex system, each component of the system has a reciprocal relationship with every other component (see box 'Types of relationships within systems', page 52).

- Feedback loops: A distinction is made between positive and negative feedback loops. In a positive feedback loop, the effect of a signal is further strengthened by the response it activates (rising salaries can lead to rising prices and thus to salaries rising even more). Positive feedback loops can drive themselves to mounting extremes and become dangerous if they are not checked by negative feedback (self-regulation). If this does not happen, the system "dies." Negative feedback slows down the triggers. In the Earth system, we can find numerous examples of positive and negative feedback loops.

- Temporal and spatial lags: Often, a cause leads to an effect only after a period of time, a time lag. In the first chapter, we gave the example of the hole in the ozone layer, caused by the emission of chlorofluorocarbons. Many years lay between the use of CFCs and the destruction of the ozone layer. Time lags often make it very difficult to link effects back to concrete causes. Countermeasures are therefore often taken (too) late.

- Vacillations: The system does not develop at a steady rate; it does not grow evenly, but in leaps and bounds, the pace becomes faster or slower, etc. A glacier does not always move at the same speed, rather it may move with a jerk, then rest for a time, and then again move more quickly.

- Uncertainties: It is not possible to predict the development of a complex system with a high degree of accuracy. Too many factors have to be taken into account: the development of the system's surroundings, the possible effects produced by changes in systems on higher or lower levels, interactions between elements. These are all reasons why developments can be predicted only within certain ranges and with only limited probability, or why they cannot be predicted at all. This also explains why weather forecasts are seldom exact. The longer the range of the forecast, the less accurate it is.

- Hierarchies: A complex system is embedded in hierarchies of other systems from above and below. As we have already mentioned, systems have different levels. One of these levels is spatial. For example, the city of Chicago is part of the state of Illinois, which in turn is part of the USA. An example of a hierarchy in a socio-economic system is a city with many schools which in turn have many students.

- Irreversibility: Processes are irreversible when they cannot be undone once they have taken place. When certain changes occur or certain limits are crossed, it is no longer possible to return to the original state. If we intervene in processes to such an extent that the systems are no longer able to fulfill their functions; when thresholds are crossed, we speak of irreversible events. The extinction of plant and animal species is an example of an irreversible process.

- Self-organization: Systems which organize themselves spontaneously change their structures and behavioral patterns. The input of energy is a precondition for the occurrence of self-organization. A well-known case of (physical) self-organization is the creation of structures in the animal kingdom such as those made by bees (on the one hand the creation of honeycomb, on the other hand the development of social structures). One example of self-organization in socio-economic systems is so-called herd behavior. It describes situations in which individuals in a group act together without any coordination among themselves; this can be easily observed at demonstrations, for example.

- Co-evolving processes: A system is in a state of constant development, it is evolving. This does not, however, take place independently of the evolution of other systems. Adaptations take place reciprocally. Above we gave the example of the forest and the humans who make use of it.

In Chapter 1, we also mentioned thresholds as part of the Earth system. We now see that some processes cause an instantaneous change in a system's behavior after a certain boundary has been crossed. It is also possible that the system collapses completely and is no longer able to keep functioning properly. Usually this momentous change does not take place at a slow and steady pace, but all at once. In a volcano, for example, molten magma bubbles and seethes for a long time below the surface, building up pressure until one day the pressure is so high that it bursts out of the volcano. Lakes are able to clean themselves to a certain degree and can break down sewage that is drained into them. However, if more and more sewage is poured into the lake, then at some point, the lake system is no longer able to maintain these functions and can no longer clean itself. The system collapses, the lake dies, and becomes water in which practically no life can exist.

Once these thresholds are crossed, there is no going back. We are witnesses to an irreversible process. Natural systems often have amazing powers of resistance and endurance and are able to function despite adverse conditions for a long time (this ability of systems is called resilience). However, it is difficult to predict how long this ability can be maintained under negative conditions and at which point it is lost and the threshold crossed.

Before the threshold is reached, the system seems not to react to the pressures that lead to the abrupt changes that take place as soon as the threshold is crossed. Because the system exhibits this seemingly limitless tolerance, warning signals are often recognized too late and it is no longer possible to react in time. This is why complex systems cannot be controlled effectively. When we influence them, or interfere with their development, the result can be either changes that are both sudden and severe, or weak (or much delayed) reactions.

We must understand that it is impossible to make predictions for complex systems for longer than limited periods of time. We can predict the regional weather for tomorrow or the coming days, but not the weather for an entire year. All the computer models, formulas, and mathematics in the world are not enough for us to completely grasp, calculate, or describe these systems. Nevertheless, we can apply scientific analysis to complex open systems. Systems theory attempts to understand such systems and their behavior and (as far as possible) to calculate and model them.

The complex Earth system

When we think about the Earth in relation to the characteristics of complex systems listed above, we recognize immediately that the Earth is a prime example of this kind of system. The Earth system and its many subsystems exhibit all characteristics of complex systems. And as with all complex systems, here, too, the system must be dealt with in a specific, appropriate manner. Human interference has far-reaching impacts and we cannot assume that they will be clear or controllable, whether our interference was "negative" or "positive."

As we have seen above, Earth is an open system, in contact with its surroundings, outer space. However, it is not a system without limits. We cannot use it forever as a sink for our wastes and emissions; both its spatial capacity and its ability to process and break down waste are limited. And of course we also cannot exploit its natural resources forever. They were created over a period of millions of years and cannot reproduce themselves in the hundreds or thousands of years that humans are taking to mine them. Since the speed at which we extract natural resources

Types of relationships within systems

(1) Linear: An effect changes to the same extent as its cause. There are very few examples of this to be found in nature. One example is the yield of corn per unit of area, which increases proportionally to the depth of the humus; but even here linearity is only given within certain bounds – if the humus layer exceeds a certain depth, the yield no longer increases.

(2) Non-linear: Cause and effect do not change to the same degree. Instead there is a mix of stasis, saturation, and acceleration. When more money is spent on research, the quality of results improves disproportionately; but after a certain amount of time saturation occurs, since quality is also dependent upon other factors (for example infrastructure or environment). A well-known example for a non-linear relationship is exponential growth (see the example of the water lily in Chapter 1). When we fail to notice such processes in time, we head towards the final limit or cross over thresholds that lead to a collapse of the system.

is higher than the rate at which they are regenerated; and the rate at which we burden Earth with waste is higher than the breakdown rate, we are upsetting the dynamic balance of Earth. We are interfering in processes without knowing or understanding what impact this will have.

Nevertheless, people have been and still are dealing with the Earth system very well in many areas. Our realization of the fact that the Earth is a complex system and that we do not know the impact of our interference is the precondition for changing our actions and our policies. Otherwise, the Earth may become imbalanced and no longer able to provide us with the basis for life and development. As the systems scientist Frederic Vester says, simple cause-and-effect thinking is not suited for treating the Earth properly or for solving our current problems, because it is geared towards individual problems. We need to be able to think in terms of dynamic structures and have an understanding of complex systems.

DPSIR — A framework for describing the environmental impact of our activities

Systemic processes, their causes, effects, and interconnections, can be described in a variety of ways. The European Environment Agency (EEA) and the United Nations Environment Programme (UNEP), as well as other institutions, use the so-called DPSIR framework. This framework helps in describing causal relationships in the environment and in social systems in order to assess appropriate political measures and behaviors.

DPSIR is an acronym: D stands for *driving force*, P for *pressure*, S for *state*, I for *impact* and R for *response*. In the following table, we explain what we mean by these terms when we use them.

Term	Explanation
driving force	refers to the driving forces of changes caused by human activities; they put pressure on systems indirectly and can be of demographic, economic, social, political, scientific, technological, or spiritual nature (e.g. the demand for energy, economic growth, the demand for food and housing, population growth).
pressure	refers to pressures and stress points that impact systems and manifest themselves as changed environmental conditions (e.g. greenhouse gas emissions, contaminated sites, noise).
state	refers to the quantitative and qualitative condition of a system (e.g. lake water quality, average global temperature, number of species in a forest).
impact	refers to the specific effect of a pressure on ecosystems' functioning and thus also on humans and their quality of life (e.g. health problems, species extinction, eutrophication).
response	refers to political and societal reactions (e.g. taxes, laws, migration) that reduce the driving forces and the pressures or make adaptation to the changed condition and its impact possible.

Figure 2.1 illustrates the individual terms and interconnectivity of the DPSIR model, using the simple example of river water quality. The starting point is the current state: the (poor) water quality. Where does it come from? It has developed due to pressures from the community's sewage, itself the result of rising population growth in communities upriver. This has an impact on human health and on the river's ability to function (for example, its regeneration capability). There are various possible responses, each of which intervenes at different points of the cycle. For example, building waste water treatment plants would stop or reduce the release of sewage into the river. Measures taken at the end of the chain, such as using bottled drinking water, are so-called end-of-pipe measures. They do not remedy

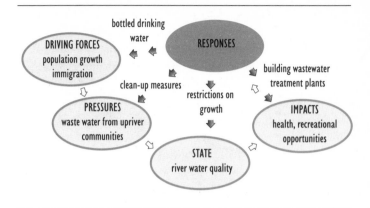

Figure 2.1 The DPSIR model explained using the example river water quality

the causes (the pressures and the driving forces), but rather minimize the effects. In principle, of course, it is better to solve the root causes of problems so that negative impacts (e.g. illness) do not arise in the first place. By removing the cause, sometimes it is even possible to solve several problems simultaneously. On the other hand, remedying the causes (for example reducing population growth) can also have negative effects (labor shortages). This example provides a vivid illustration of the importance of examining all elements within a larger context when solving complex problems, so as to be as sure as possible that the point at which one intervenes will bring about the most effective outcomes.

The DPSIR framework attempts to provide information for each element of the DPSIR chain, demonstrate their interconnectedness, and estimate the effectiveness of responses. It connects causes (driving forces and pressures) to states, activities (policy measures and decisions), and the impact on humans.

This model is an extreme simplification of systemic processes, for which reason it is also often criticized. Admittedly, it is only *one* method among many others of describing systemic problems. However, since it demonstrates the interconnectedness of natural systems and socio-economic systems and thus can also help pinpoint where measures are desired and necessary, it is a method of representation which serves the purposes of this chapter well. Nevertheless, it is important to always be conscious of the fact that the DPSIR framework is not able to demonstrate the complexity of all interconnections and thus should not be the only model used as a problem-solving aid.

After this excursion into the somewhat abstract world of systems and systems theory, in the following we shall demonstrate the complexity of existing interconnections with the help of three examples of human-induced changes in the Earth system. In doing so, we use the terms described above. When we do not use them directly, we have added them in parentheses.

Climate change

Let us take a look at climate change as our first example. Influenced by factors which span the globe, the Earth's climate system in turn causes global changes and is a prime example of complexity (one of the books in this series, Mojib Latif's *Climate Change: The Point of No Return,* deals exclusively with climate change). According to UNEP (1999), climate change will be the most important environmental problem in the future by far; a claim supported by the almost daily appearance of newspaper articles on the subject. Only very few scientists still deny that we are currently undergoing climate change and that it is caused by human activity. The issue raises a multitude of questions: What will the consequences be? Are the ceilings set in the Kyoto Protocol sufficient to reduce impacts to a bearable level? Does it even make sense to work towards reaching Kyoto Protocol reduction goals when important countries aren't doing their part and the carbon dioxide emissions of many threshold countries with large populations are rising sharply?

Let us look at the individual factors one by one. What are the pressures and driving forces leading to climate change (state)? The gas most relevant for climate change is carbon dioxide. For millions of years, it has been part of our atmosphere – in and of itself, it is harmless. What is more, life on Earth was only able to develop in its current diversity due to the capacity of carbon dioxide to store heat in the atmosphere. Short-wave (ultraviolet) radiation from the Sun passes through this atmospheric gas unhindered, whereas the long-wave radiation sent back from the Earth's surface is absorbed by carbon dioxide and other greenhouse gases. Thus the Earth retains part of the sun's warmth; without carbon dioxide, the average temperature on Earth would be -18° centigrade instead of +15° centigrade. This mechanism is called the greenhouse effect. In the past decades, however, the level of carbon dioxide in the atmosphere has been rising continuously.

How scientists were able to figure out the connection between CO_2 and the climate can be illustrated by an example from Antarctica. At the Vostok research site near the magnetic South Pole, scientists were able to drill and analyze a long ice core (see Petit et al.). Since ice is formed year by year by the compression of layers of snow, it is possible to distinguish annual layers of ice. One can also determine the age of the ice layers and the concentration of certain atmospheric gases at the time of the snowfall, as these gases remain trapped in small bubbles in the ice. By measuring particular oxygen isotopes, Earth's temperature at the time the ice was formed can also be determined. Through painstaking detailed work, the scientists were thus able to reconstruct the history of the Earth system. Figure 2.2 shows the atmospheric concentration of carbon dioxide and methane as well as the temperature over a period of slightly more than 400,000 years.

In this 'Vostok curve,' the similarity between changes in carbon dioxide and methane levels on the one hand and temperature on the other is immediately noticeable. Their rise and fall is almost simultaneous. The lowest levels of gas concentrations and temperature are found during the four major ice ages around 20,000 years ago, 150,000 years ago, 270,000 years ago, and 340,000 years ago. This illustrates a relatively stable cycle of approximately 100,000 years, which coincides with changes in the orbit of the Earth around the Sun. However, changes in the orbit alone are too small and too regular to offer a full explanation of these curves. Particularly the abrupt warming after an ice age points towards a complex interaction of atmosphere, oceans, and biosphere.

What is also very interesting is the fact that the values lie within an almost constant range. The maximum values of all interglacial periods reach roughly the same high level and the minimum values reach more or less the same low level in all ice ages. In other words, the Earth system regulated itself. Interactions between the atmosphere, the oceans, and the biosphere ensured regular cycles.

Let us go back to the Vostock ice core and look at the concentrations of carbon dioxide measured there in comparison to measurements made in the atmosphere in the past fifty years. (The first regular measurements of atmospheric carbon dioxide were begun in 1957 in Hawaii; see Keeling and Whorf). Since emissions are scattered quickly by atmospheric circulation, measurements from one point on Earth supply sufficient evidence for worldwide

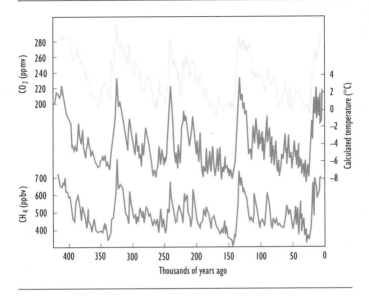

Figure 2.2 Measurements of carbon dioxide and methane levels as well
as temperature in the Antarctic ice
The curves show the four ice ages and interglacial periods over the past 420,000 years.

concentrations. Figure 2.3 illustrates this comparison. It shows
the carbon dioxide concentration levels of the past 420,000 years
measured in the Vostok ice core and the concentration levels of
the past fifty years at measurement stations at the Earth's surface.
Whereas the concentration levels of carbon dioxide in the atmosphere fluctuated between 100 and 280 ppm over a period of
420,000 years, in the past fifty years the concentration levels have
risen by almost 100 ppm, measuring approximately 370 ppm in
the year 2000. Without a doubt, human activities have caused
the concentration of carbon dioxide to rise way above the levels
which have been natural for the past 420,000 years.

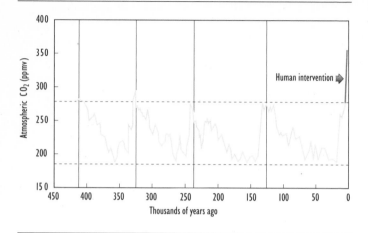

Figure 2.3 The concentration of carbon dioxide in the atmosphere over the past 420,000 years, measured in the Vostok ice core

In comparison, measurements of concentrations in recent years. Today's levels can be seen at the right side of the curve.

The main pressure is the combustion of enormous amounts of fossil energy carriers (coal, natural gas, and mineral oil). Through this, in the past decades humans have released into the atmosphere masses of carbon dioxide that were previously contained below the surface of the Earth (see Hermann-Josef Wagner's book in this series on the topic of energy use). The deforestation of large areas also contributes to rising levels of carbon dioxide, because the carbon stored in the wood is freed as soon as the wood is burned or rots.

Further pressures from human activities are connected to other greenhouse gases. Carbon dioxide is perhaps the most important, but not the only greenhouse gas. The six greenhouse gases whose emissions are to be limited by the Kyoto Protocol are: carbon dioxide, methane, nitrous oxide (laughing gas, N_2O), hydrofluorocarbons (HFCs), perfluorocarbons (PFCs), and sulfur hexaflouride (SF_6). Hydrofluorocarbons are alternatives to the CFCs banned by the Montreal Protocol. They are less destructive to stratospheric ozone than CFCs, but they intensify the greenhouse effect. Methane creates a much stronger greenhouse effect than carbon dioxide and is released into the atmosphere by livestock breeding, rice cultivation, and waste-disposal dumps. The consumption of fossil fuels, rampant deforestation, livestock breeding (stimulated by rising meat consumption), and rice cultivation all increase with the growth of the population and the economy as well as with the rise in trade that accompanies globalization. The main causes of climate change are therefore an energy policy focused on fossil fuels and non-sustainable lifestyles. These can be identified as the primary driving forces behind the rising levels of greenhouse gas concentrations.

The increased concentration of carbon dioxide and other gases in the atmosphere intensifies the greenhouse effect. This results in an increase in the Earth's average temperature (state). Scientists have worked out a variety of scenarios to show how the carbon dioxide concentration and Earth's average temperature might develop. The Intergovernmental Panel on Climate Change (IPCC), an international committee of scientists who evaluate all aspects of climate change at regular intervals and report to the governments of the world, estimates a rise in global temperature between 1.4 and 5.8°C in the period from 1990 to 2100.

There have always been changes in our climate. What is new, however, is that the changes currently occurring are caused by a rising concentration of greenhouse gases that can be traced back to human activities (driving forces) at levels higher than they have ever been in recent geological history. Furthermore, the speed at which these man-made changes take place is unusually high.

Human-induced climate change is a widely accepted state. But what is so bad about it? Particularly in northern countries, many people think that milder winters and warmer summers might be pretty nice. However, climate change is a good example of the complex interconnections between the atmosphere, the biosphere, and the oceans as well as between these natural systems and socio-economic systems. Rising temperatures are not the only issue. When we take a closer look, we can quickly see that we can't just "order" better weather by raising our carbon dioxide emissions. The effects of climate change are manifold, we are still not able to project many of them, and it remains unclear whether there will be any 'winners' of climate change.

These interconnections have been researched only in the past few decades. Even if some of this knowledge now seems very familiar to us, in the main these insights are relatively new.

What are the results of rising temperatures? Let's begin with rising sea levels, which can already be observed. Their main cause is the expansion of water. Water's density is highest at 4° centigrade – therefore, at this temperature, the most water fits into a defined volume. Should water temperatures rise, the water will expand and need more space. The ocean will spill over like a full glass, spreading out over what had formerly been land. Over the past 6000 years, the sea level has risen by a maximum of one millimeter – usually less – annually; we know this from geological data. In the 20th century, however, the sea level began to rise more quickly: by one to two millimeters per year. For each centimeter the sea rises, around one meter of coastal land is lost to the ocean. At the current rate, therefore, we must be prepared for the loss of one meter every five to ten years.

Model calculations assume that the sea level will rise up to ninety centimeters by the year 2100. The average projected increase lies at forty-nine centimeters in the year 2100 (IPCC,

2001). In the worst case, the figure will be much higher. Flat coastal areas in particular will be affected most. Figure 2.4 shows the impact of a 1.5 meter rise in the sea level on Bangladesh. It would result in the flooding of 22,000 square kilometers of land and 17 million people would lose their homes (IPCC). The people living in the affected areas would either be forced to migrate or would have to be protected from the sea by highly complex technical devices; the coastal areas, economically important for tourism and harbors, would be equally affected. Fresh water reserves would dwindle because salt water would penetrate the ground water reserves; individual animal and plant species as well as entire ecosystems would become extinct. While this is only a partial list of possible effects, it already shows how diverse the impacts of pressures can be. Humans as well as plants and animals would be affected – even if we like to think we are superior to nature.

A further important reason for rising sea levels (state) is the melting of the polar ice sheets, another result of increasing temperatures. The following numbers give an idea of the dimensions of the problem: if the Greenland ice sheet melts, it would lead to a rise of three to six meters, the melting of the Western Antarctic ice sheet would cause a rise of further three meters (see Flannery).

The example of glaciers possibly melting once again clearly shows the complexity of climate change – rising sea levels are not the only consequence by far. White glacial surfaces reflect much of the sun's radiation back into space. Its warmth is thus lost. Glacial retreat would also cause a decrease in the reflection of solar energy into space and an increase in the absorption of the sun's rays. The energy would thus remain in Earth's energy system – a further contribution to global warming and a strong positive feedback loop. Anyone can produce this effect

EFFECTS OF RISING SEA LEVELS ON BANGLADESH

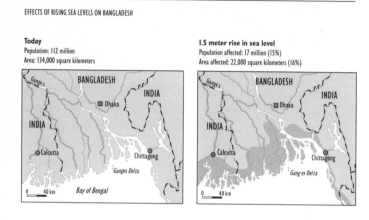

Today
Population: 112 million
Area: 134,000 square kilometers

1.5 meter rise in sea level
Population affected: 17 million (15%)
Area affected: 22,000 square kilometers (16%)

Figure 2.4 Impact on Bangladesh of a 1.5-meter rise in the sea level

themselves. All you need to do is sit in the sun on a warm clear summer day in a dark t-shirt. Dark areas absorb sunlight. Therefore a person dressed in dark clothes will suffer more from the sun than one dressed in light clothes. We can expect a similar effect should large areas of what is now land be flooded – this, too, would cause changes in the reflection of heat into space.

In addition to the effects of climate change described above, an increase in the average temperature of Earth would also change amounts and patterns of precipitation. These changes are very difficult to predict, but such changes were already observed in the 20th century. Figure 2.5 shows that precipitation has increased in northern latitudes (for example in the north of Norway, Sweden, and Canada) and decreased in the tropics (particularly south of the Sahara). Rises in temperature cause a change in the air's ability to absorb water vapor, accelerating the hydrologic cycle. One should not, however, make the general assumption that it will rain more. Rather, the effects may vary greatly from region to region. In some regions it will rain more, in others it will be drier (it seems likely that this will occur in those areas with little rain today). Meteorologists predict an increase in extreme weather events such as droughts, floods, hurricanes, etc.

A further impact is changes in global ocean currents. Currents are dependent upon the ocean's temperature and salinity, which also change when evaporation increases. One possible consequence is that the Gulf Stream may be reduced or even shut down completely. In contrast to rising temperatures around the world, this would lead to an extreme cooling in Europe, because the Gulf Stream brings Europe warm air from the South (for a detailed discussion of this topic, see Katherine Richardson and Stefan Rahmstorf's book in this series, *Our Threatened Oceans*).

One example of a positive feedback loop (a cycle which reinforces itself) is the connection between rising temperatures and the marine absorption of carbon dioxide (see Richardson). Scientists formerly believed that higher temperatures caused a higher rate of photosynthesis (the absorption of carbon dioxide from the air); new research has shown that, to the contrary, biological activity decreases. Furthermore, due to higher water temperatures, the oceans emit more carbon dioxide.

Changing temperatures alter the habitats of all living creatures. One cannot, however, assume, that animals and plants will migrate with "their" temperature zone (meaning that plants that formerly existed only further south will migrate to central Europe, or that the timber line will be higher). For this to happen, many conditions would have to be met – it does not help that the temperature is right if the vegetation to which the animal has adapted for its food source no longer exists; or when seeds are spread into the right temperature zone, but land on the wrong

TREND OF ANNUAL PRECIPITATION (1900–2000)

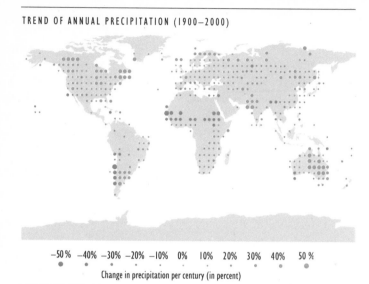

−50% −40% −30% −20% −10% 0% 10% 20% 30% 40% 50%

Change in precipitation per century (in percent)

Figure 2.5 Global changes in precipitation in the 20th century

soil. Some animal and plant species will become extinct as a result of climate change. At the same time, (undesirable) organisms such as pathogens will move into areas where the conditions they needed were previously lacking.

A further feedback loop in the climate system that will become very important is caused by warming in the North. Northern areas exhibit a high proportion of permafrost, which contains large amounts of methane hydrate – as does the ocean floor. Methane hydrate is methane which is trapped in frozen water. As mentioned above, methane is a much stronger greenhouse gas than CO_2. It presents a further risk for our climate. Should the permafrost thaw in the course of global warming, it may cause a sudden release of methane, which in turn could cause an unpredictable acceleration of global warming. This example shows how crossing a (still unknown) threshold can cause an abrupt change. It also illustrates the impact of positive feedback loops.

Therefore, when looking at climate change, we must remember that the interconnections between individual factors are complex and diverse and the consequences can vary greatly. The sensitivity and the ability of both the Earth system and human beings to adapt are not equally pronounced in all cases and all places. This discussion is therefore riddled with open questions.

One can divide the reactions and responses to climate change into two groups. First, reducing the greenhouse effect by reducing greenhouse gas emissions, and second, the adaptation of organisms to climate change. The first can be achieved by switching to renewable energy sources, by increasing energy efficiency, and by saving energy. In concrete terms this entails, for example, using public transportation and bicycles instead of cars and not flying (on this see also Hermann-Josef Wagner, *Energy: The World's Race for Resources in the 21st Century*). For this to happen, we need appropriate energy policy, and we need to raise public awareness. In animals and plants, adaptation occurs through migration or, in the long-term, through mutations. Humans can also migrate or put in air conditioning (which further exacerbates the greenhouse effect); they can make sure they do not build houses in areas prone to flooding, etc. These examples alone make clear that adaptation is much easier for the rich of the world than for people in developing countries.

The Lake Victoria perch story

Our second example examines a very different problem. It describes the manifold and unforeseeable results of a small human interference in one region's ecosystem and social system: stocking Lake Victoria in Africa with non-native Nile perch. This story is also an example of very complex interconnections (see Fuggle for a detailed description). Not all of the resulting impacts can be traced directly to the release of the Nile perch, but they are connected to it. But let us start from the beginning.

Lake Victoria borders Kenya, Tanzania, and Uganda and is the largest lake in Africa. It is about the same size as Ireland. Until well into the 20th century, strict social conventions ensured that the lake was not overfished. Problems began when the population rose due to better transportation infrastructure and higher agricultural yields, and the need for fish rich in protein increased accordingly (driving force). Due to more efficient fishing methods (drift gillnets), many native species were over-fished; particularly those fish which ate algae and rotting plant material. As the fish stocks dwindled, people began to think about finding alternatives. In 1960, Nile perch (*Lates niloticus*) were released into Lake Victoria (pressure) despite forceful pro-tests by many scientists who feared that the Nile perch could negatively impact the lake's ecosystem because it is a predatory fish that would eat the native fish. The driving forces in this case were economic goals and the hope that Lake Victoria perch (as Nile perch was called after it was released) would meet the protein needs of the larger population.

Lates niloticus is a very good and nutritious edible fish. It can be found on the markets of Europe, the USA, Japan, and other rich countries under the name Lake Victoria perch and is quite popular. In this respect, the Lake Victoria perch story is an economic success story. When the Lake Victoria stocks had grown enough, many commercial fishing companies were founded; they also packed the fish hygienically and exported it to the rich target countries. Foreign investment flowed into the countries bordering on Lake Victoria; new roads were built, the aviation industry boomed, the balance of trade tipped towards surplus.

But a high price was paid for this economic success. Today, the native tilapia has been made almost completely extinct by the predatory Lake Victoria perch, and the lake water has become very unclean due to algae and pollution. There have also been negative social effects. Many of the fishermen, who used to fish for themselves and whose wives sold the fish on local markets, now work for the new companies. Their income, however, is usually not high enough to be able to buy the fish – which has become very expensive due to the export industry – for themselves. The results have been malnutrition and undernourishment. The situation is exacerbated by the fact that the large Lake Victoria perch, in contrast to the native tilapia, cannot be dried. Since refrigeration is not an option, preserving fish is difficult for the local population. Furthermore, women have lost their direct access to the catch, because the fishing companies tend to hire men. The population on the shores of Lake Victoria today must live off the leftovers of the exported fish – skeletons with almost nothing edible left on them.

The situation for the lakeshore societies is made even worse by the fact that the region has one of the highest rates of HIV/AIDS in Africa – the proportion of twenty to forty-year-old men on the boats has dropped rapidly. Saturday, the traditional day for funerals, is no longer long enough. The spread of the virus is sustained by cultural traditions which are difficult to combat. They include a widespread refusal to use condoms, traditional sexual practices favorable to the spread of the virus, and the belief that AIDS is not caused by a virus, but by violating taboos. Furthermore – and all these factors have a negative impact on one another – the social situation also contributes to the spread of the virus. Poor women try to support themselves by prostitution; their clients, the many men working as fishermen far from their families, carry the virus into the villages.

The economic success story does not add these costs to the bill – the costs of lacking food security, of malnutrition, disease, and the transformation of the local economy.

Nor does the story end here. Parallel to the fish industry boom, there was also a surge in the cultivation of coffee and tea on the banks of the headwaters of the tributaries. This is also an export-oriented industry – at the recommendation of the World Bank and development organizations – because income generated can be used to pay off debt. And directly on the lakeshore, more rice and sugar cane was cultivated, all using intensive fertilization. This resulted in more and more nutrients being added to the lake, and phytoplankton growth exploded. This further endangered the native fish species, as the clear water essential to them became more and more clouded by the plankton. Thus the native fish were subjected to two negative developments: the predatory Lake Victoria perch and the plankton.

As if that were not enough, the nutrient contamination from agriculture and the inflow of untreated sewage from the surrounding communities provided the perfect conditions for a further plague which now threatens the lake and also the fishing industry: the water hyacinth. The water hyacinth originated in Brazil and is one of the most dangerous invasive species in the world. This is the designation for species which do not originally come from a region, but thrive there and so change the original ecosystem. Water hyacinths can float freely or they can put in roots, and they can cover the water's surface. In warm water with a lot of nutrients, they reproduce at an amazing rate: within ten to twenty days, the overgrown area can double in size (compare our calculation of the growth of the water lily in Chapter 1). The fact is, these plants curb the economy enormously, since small boats and canoes are no longer able to go out to fish – and they are even a serious encumbrance to large ships. Activity at entire harbors grinds to a halt when the wind blows the free-floating water hyacinths into them. Fighting the water hyacinth is a very difficult and expensive procedure.

The driving forces behind these changes, interconnections, and unexpected effects were economic goals, as mentioned above. The impacts are eutrophication and the displacement of other life-forms from the lake; furthermore, the livelihoods of many inhabitants were destroyed. Responses include measures to clean up the lake. Hubert Sauper's film *Darwin's Nightmare*, which tells this story in vivid and forceful images, must also be considered an example of a social response because he brought the situation of Lake Victoria into the public consciousness and thus improved the chances of obtaining international support.

In the meantime, many programs have been started to improve the water quality and to gain control of the spread of the water hyacinth. These programs are expensive, and it is as yet unclear how successful they will be. Lake Victoria is a striking example of how historic developments, agricultural practices, the fishing industry, and cultural factors all intertwine to create a very complex picture. Furthermore, these developments are not guided by the local population alone. Instead, crucial decisions are often made far away in Europe, the United States, or by international institutions.

A dam in Ghana

Our final example shows the interconnectedness between the driving force of economic development, the pressure of building a reservoir, and the resulting changes in the services provided by the ecosystem (state) as well as the impact on the prosperity of the population, and the societal responses.

The main driving force was the increased need for electricity for both industry and households in Ghana in the 1960s. There was also a need for better irrigation in Ghana's agriculture and for improving means of transportation on the river. The third and final goal was attracting tourists. All of this was to be achieved by building a dam on the Volta River in Akosombo, Ghana. In the 1960s, the largest artificial lake in the world was created; it covered almost four percent of Ghana's acreage and had a shoreline of 4800 kilometers.

But what were the ecological and social impacts of the dam? The economic advantages for this African country were restricted to a small fraction of the population. Otherwise, the dam created ecological problems as well as health issues and social problems.

The flow rate of the river below the dam decreased noticeably, causing changes in the ecology of the entire river region. Plants were able to take root which nurtured the propagation of a certain type of snail, which in turn carries intestinal and urethral illnesses. Impurities in the water caused by the snail infestation led to epidemics.

In the floodplains below the dam, less sediment was deposited in important agricultural areas; a disadvantage for local farmers. Further problems arose at the mouth of the Volta River at the Atlantic. Since there was less water flowing below the dam, salt water from the sea was able to flow upriver into the Volta.

Since the river carried less sand to the sea, the coastline moved inland. These changes destroyed the livelihoods of fishermen and farmers in the coastal area.

One response to the negative impact on health was the development of an integrated management system for the lake (see Gordon and Ametekpor). Plants were removed from the river to reduce the snail plague and with it the threat to human health. Moreover, countermeasures were taken consisting of medication and programs to improve health awareness.

The Akosombo Dam most certainly contributed to Ghana's economic development; but if one takes all of the harmful impacts into account, the final outcome is negative.

This example elucidates interconnections which can be found in many other regions of the world. Between 1950 and 1990 alone, 35,000 dams were built. The Three Gorges Dam currently under completion in China is one of the most well-known and controversial examples, due to its size and the current debates surrounding it.

Summary: systemic approaches

We now know that the Earth is an interconnected system. Even if it will never be possible to decode this system completely, we need to understand it better if we want to control the impact of our actions. The results of our behavior are manifold; they often appear at a later point in time, are unpredictable, and can thus also not be planned for entirely. Natural and socio-economic systems have a certain resiliency which helps them to bear or mitigate negative effects; however, its powers are not infinite. When thresholds are crossed, the system, or parts thereof, can fall apart. When it does, there is usually no turning back. Below are some guidelines on how we can act to prevent natural and socio-economic systems from reaching an irreversible negative state. These guidelines are intended for each and every individual. On the other hand, many of the human-induced changes in the Earth system are caused by groups or by socio-economic systems. We therefore need to create rules and regulations for these systems which ensure that they too act according to the following guidelines.

– The precautionary principle. Acting according to the precautionary principle means acting strategically and refraining from activities which contain possible risks; or changing our activities to lessen the likelihood of possible risks. Due to the complexity of systems within which human activity takes place, it is not possible to predict all impacts exactly, or they do not occur in the manner predicted. This factor of uncertainty often induces critics to reject calls to be more careful and more circumspect in our dealings with the Earth system as unfounded. Usually, economic interests are behind this carefree attitude, as the precautionary principle is an obstacle to unchecked economic growth. Experience has shown, however, that human well-being increases with an increase of precaution (for an excellent introduction to the precautionary principle, see *Late lessons from early warnings: the precautionary principle 1896–2002*, published in 2002 by the European Environment Agency).
Therefore, even if possible negative effects have not been proven (e.g. Gulf Stream shutdown), the driving forces must be minimized. This is the only way we can be sure that we will not cause unwanted results which affect us or coming generations. We can not end all impacts upon the Earth system – but we can try to mitigate them as much as possible.

– Since we have already influenced the Earth system
  irreversibly, many undesired impacts have already become
  reality. In these cases, it is not enough to act according the
  precautionary principle, but it is necessary to take measures
  which reduce negative impacts – measures which help people
  and natural systems to adapt (e.g. support for relocation
  into an area which is not prone to flooding). All efforts to
  reduce further negative impacts are also helpful, such as a
  tax on carbon dioxide or supporting renewable energy.
– To take the multiple causes of problems fully into account,
  it is important not to enact individual political measures,
  but to take an integrated approach. Individual measures
  may lead to the intended effect, but they may also impact
  negatively on other areas. In contrast, integrated means
  "adapted to the system and its interconnections." Such
  measures require not only a profound knowledge of the
  system; due to their complexity, they can also take a lot of
  time and be difficult to implement.
  The chances of successful problem-solving increase when
  the people affected participate in developing solutions.
  When the knowledge and the desires of the population and
  other stakeholders are taken into account, strategies are
  better grounded in reality and are more likely to be accepted
  by those affected by the problem. Furthermore, through
  participation, people are able to become fully conscious of
  the complexity of a problem.
– Interconnections therefore not only make finding a solution
  to a problem more difficult, they can also improve its
  chances of success. When we have understood the structures
  and processes of a system, targeted measures can achieve
  multiple positive results. We can, so to speak, work with
  the power of the opponent, as in many Asian martial arts

("ju-jitsu principle"). It is often sufficient to make only one change in order to solve many problems. Reducing traffic, for example, contributes to the reduction of greenhouse gas emissions as well as to a reduction in noise and accidents and an improvement in air quality, etc.

3 Resource Use – We're Living Beyond Our Means

In light of the interconnections of the Earth system described above, it is clear that "environmental problems" cannot be understood as isolated individual events; rather they present a challenge to the entire system of humans and our environment. Therefore, suitable responses to these challenges should not focus on individual problems either, but always on the entire system. It's all or nothing! This is why we need a comprehensive view of the totality of all human-induced changes to the ecosphere. That is the focus of this chapter.

Humans are part of nature

Natural resources in the form of material and energy, as well as the area available to us on Earth, are the basis of all life processes on our planet. We humans are also part of nature. Without the permanent utilization of natural resources, neither the economy nor society could function. Nature provides humans with all resources necessary for life: energy for heat, electricity, and mobility; wood for furniture and paper products; cotton for clothing; construction materials for our roads and houses; food and pure water for a healthy life. However, every use of resources means intervening in natural cycles. Intervention is not problematic *per se*, but as we have seen it is not always easy (in fact, it is often completely impossible) to predict all environmental impacts. From the perspective of sustainability, the general rule is therefore to interfere with natural processes as little as possible. The following chapters (4 and 5) show that by no means must this have a negative effect on "the good life."

To get an overview of human-made impacts on the complex Earth system, in the following we have reduced them to relatively simple numbers: the total amount of land or resources used by one person, one product, one city, or even one entire country.

One way of visualizing this is to think of nature as "capital" used by humans to produce what they need to exist. In economics, "capital" usually only denotes the financial means necessary for production; sometimes, it also includes machines, buildings, and streets. Too often, the fact is overlooked that in the end it is nature that provides us with all "means of production." Since nature costs little or nothing, people often limit their description of the functioning of the economy to labor and capital.

The stock of natural resources as well as ecosystems with their networks of the environment, plants, and animals, are known as "Natural Capital" (see box "Natural Capital").

Like living creatures, economies and societies can be regarded as a large "organism" through which energy and materials flow. Raw materials are extracted from nature, then transformed into "goods" utilizable by people, and finally returned to the natural system as waste. Every city and every country therefore has a "metabolism," just like every plant, animal, or person. This exchange of material and energy between a social system and nature is known as a "social metabolism" (Fig. 3.1).

Social metabolisms have changed dramatically in the course of human history. They have grown more than ten-fold from the Stone Age until today. The cultural development of mankind is also the history of an ever more efficient exploitation of natural

Natural Capital

Natural capital refers to all areas of nature and ecosystems that provide goods and services to people. These goods include renewable raw materials and food such as water, wood, grain, and fish. Furthermore, people also take non-renewable raw materials from nature, such as fossil fuels (coal, crude oil, natural gas), minerals, and metal ores.

Renewable resources are constantly available to people – as long as the extent of their use does not exceed nature's regenerative capacity. The amount of non-renewable resources, on the other hand, is reduced each time they are extracted. Some materials, such as metals or building materials, can be partially – but never entirely – recycled, in order to make them usable for humans again.

In addition to goods, natural capital also provides us with a variety of services. These include a stable climate, forests that protect us from soil erosion, and the ozone layer that protects us from damaging ultraviolet radiation. For nature to be able to continue to provide these services, and also to continually regenerate itself, the structure and diversity of ecosystems must remain intact.

capital. Early social systems such as those of hunter-gatherers as well as early agrarian societies (with cultivation of land and animal husbandry), from the Egyptians to the Middle Ages, were mainly dependent upon the use of renewable natural resources such as wood, water, and solar energy. However, a certain area of land was only able to provide a certain amount of energy and

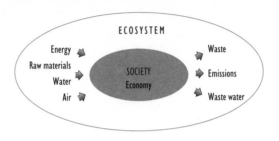

Figure 3.1 Social metabolism

food. This fact also limited the growth of the population and of the economy.

A hunter-gatherer had a per capita consumption of natural resources of about one metric ton per year, used mostly for food, basic housing, and weapons for bringing down prey. In agrarian societies, consumption already rose to three to five metric tons per year. A large percentage of this upsurge, in comparison to hunter-gatherer societies, was due to the increased need for feed for animals kept for milk and meat production. At the same time, larger buildings were erected, and more metallic objects, such as plows, weapons, and cooking pots, were produced.

The Industrial Revolution in the 18th century launched the most important change in the social metabolism to date, one that still has bearing on our development. With the use of fossil fuels (at first coal, as of the 20th century also crude oil and natural gas), suddenly much more energy, in comparison to earlier societal forms, was available to mankind. The dependency on wood, which is always extracted from a limited area, as the most important source of energy came to an end. Driven by this energy thrust, societies began to change more dynamically in fifty years than in the previous thousand years of human history.

The use of fossil fuels produced over millions of years created an energy surplus for mankind, the precondition for the economic growth that has continued until today. It was the availability of energy in a cheaper and more concentrated form that allowed the sharp increase in the production of goods. The population has also grown steadily since the Industrial Revolution, because the use of ever more machines and ever greater amounts of fertilizer caused a constant increase in harvest yields per unit of area. Therefore, one hectare of arable land today feeds many more people than it did in agrarian societies, which were limited to the use of human and animal labor and had no chemical fertilizers. However, progress had its price: the consumption of resources rose dramatically. One resident of an industrialized country today uses fifteen to thirty-five metric tons of raw materials and products annually (not counting their "ecological rucksacks," explained further on in this chapter) – in comparison to agrarian societies, a five- to ten-fold increase!

The use of natural capital is also the topic of Klaus Hahlbrock's book in this series, *Feeding the Planet: Environmental Protection through Sustainable Agriculture*. Hahlbrock delineates the need for an agriculture that combines high productivity with lower environmental impact and the long-term protection of species, water, the soil, and our climate. His analysis of realistic options concentrates on the dual question of whether this goal can be reached by the further development of plant genetic engineering, and under which conditions the use of genetic engineering can be justified.

The environmental problems faced by different societal forms have also changed in the course of human history. In hunter-gatherer societies as well as in agrarian societies, the greatest challenge, in terms of environmental sustainability, was not to overuse the renewable resources available in the region. This was achieved, among other things, by cultural norms. These included dietary restrictions such as fasting, or taboos on certain types of meat (pork in Islam and beef in Hinduism) that limited the consumption of animal protein. Like people, pigs eat a large variety of foods and therefore compete with humans for scarce resources. Population growth itself was also controlled. Long periods of breastfeeding and preaching abstinence caused longer intervals between births. Furthermore, a large percentage of the population was excluded from reproducing, because, for example, only the heir to the farm was allowed to marry.

When these restrictions failed, the result was ecological collapse, as the striking example of Easter Island demonstrates. There, a range of activities led to the overexploitation of the natural foundation of the population's existence; in particular, erecting the world-famous stone figures and clearing the palm forests for wood and new farmland. The destruction of the ecological foundation of human existence led to food scarcity, and finally – as Jared Diamond so vividly describes – to the demise of Easter Island's economy and culture. This story holds a lesson for us: just as the inhabitants of Easter Island could not flee, so, too, are we unable to leave our planet when we have damaged its natural systems. In addition to the overexploitation of raw materials, today's industrial societies are increasingly confronted by another type of environmental problem. We overstrain our ecosystems, making them less and less able to absorb the waste produced by people. Humans today produce many materials that either do not exist at all in natural cycles (for example plastics and certain chemicals such as CFCs), or only in small amounts (for example heavy metals). It is therefore not surprising that nature is unable, or only very slowly able, to render the waste made up of these materials harmless. The increased greenhouse effect and resulting climate change are good examples of the negative impacts our social metabolism have on nature.

Most of the currently pressing environmental problems result from the fact that the consumption of energy and raw materials, the production of waste and emissions, and the human use of land area have increased dramatically – in a timeframe of only a few decades. The growth of the world's population and the global economy seem to be unstoppable, and with them human-kind's consumption of nature. It would help us tremendously if global ecosystems would grow accordingly – but we cannot change the size of our planet. Therefore, there is only a limited natural space available for human activities, our so-called "Environmental Space" (see box below). If we use more than is available to us, we damage natural systems.

Friedrich Schmidt-Bleek already pointed out in 1993 that sustainability can only be achieved if we reduce the average global consumption of natural materials, including energy, by at least half. He refers to the space we have within the limits set by nature as "ecological corridors." Nature's goods and services and our dealings with them are the subject of Friedrich Schmidt-Bleek's book in this series, *The Earth: Natural Resources and Human Intervention*.

Under current conditions, as the increase of environmental problems illustrates, we are getting alarmingly close to the limits of what our global environmental space can endure. In some areas, we have already crossed these limits. Herman Daly, a famous American sustainability researcher, described this development as the transition from an "empty world" to a "full world;" Figure 3.2 is his graphic portrayal of this development.

To achieve sustainable development, humans must thus learn to work and live within the limits that nature sets, or, in Schmidt-

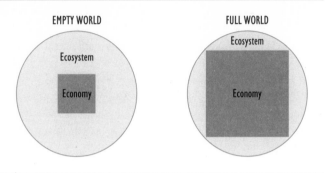

Figure 3.2 The empty world and the full world

Bleek's words, within the "ecological corridors." We can also put it another way: we must learn to live off the "interest" of the available natural capital, not off the capital itself! This means we must not exploit the goods and services nature provides us faster than they can regenerate themselves. In the case of renewable resources; humans must clear only as much wood in one year as can grow again in the following year; catch only as many fish as can reproduce in the world's oceans; etc. In the case of non-renewable resources, as a general rule, we should not use them up more rapidly than the time we need to develop and implement long-term renewable alternatives to these resources. Furthermore, living off the "interest" of natural capital also means reducing the production of waste and hazardous substances to a degree that allows them to be absorbed and processed by natural systems. This is equally true for the emissions of greenhouse gases such as carbon dioxide and for the production of municipal and industrial wastes and wastewater.

In the past fifteen years, a discussion has sprung up among scientists on the question of the extent to which natural capital can be replaced by man-made capital (such as houses, roads, machines, etc.). Followers of so-called "weak sustainability" support the position that a society is sustainable if the sum total of its capital (natural capital and man-made capital) does not decrease over time. Following this logic, it is sufficient to replace lost natural capital with man-made capital. If a forest is cleared, for example, one only needs to build a sawmill of the same economic value as the forest in order to reinstate the balance.

Followers of "weak sustainability" do not, however, take into account that one can only replace natural capital with man-made capital to a very limited extent. After all, in most cases, the production of man-made capital is dependent upon the availability of natural resources. "Strong sustainability," on the other hand, postulates that natural capital may never be depleted to a great extent, regardless of the amount of man-made capital. Nature is the foundation of our economy and our society and can not just be traded in.

Let us take a closer look at the sawmill example: The forest and wood industry is only able to generate income if there are forests that can be cleared. Moreover, forests fulfill a variety of functions which the economy neither takes into account nor could replace – for example: protection from floods, climate stabilization, and the conservation of animal and plant biodiversity.

In agriculture as well, it is very clear how fundamental "strong sustainability" is, because chemical fertilizers cannot indefinitely replace the natural fertility of soils. Almost a quarter of the arable land on our planet has already been overused by humans to an extent that its productivity is permanently falling. Humankind must therefore convert to agricultural forms that place less strain on the land (such as organic farming), to ensure that the loss of fertile topsoil (soil erosion) comes to an end. According to Klaus Hahlbrock, this necessitates harmonizing agriculture and environmental protection to a much greater extent; by increasing attention to ecological concerns and also by improving the integration of chemical, mechanical, and biological processes of fertilization and pest management. To achieve this, great hopes are placed in plant breeding. If we do not reach this goal, the developing countries will soon experience even greater scarcity than they have had to contend with to date.

How we use nature: facts and figures

Which natural resources are extracted from the deposits found around the globe? These resources include fossil fuels (coal, crude oil, natural gas), metal ores, construction materials (gravel, sand, etc.), and biomass from the agricultural, forestry, and fishing industries. If we compile these data for all countries, the sum is the resource consumption of the entire global economy.

According to these data, the extraction of natural resources has intensified worldwide in recent decades. In 1980, almost forty billion metric tons were extracted from the global ecosystem. By 2005, global use had risen to more than fifty-seven billion metric tons – by no less than one-third in only twenty-five years. The largest proportion of these resources in terms of their amount (around 40%) was for construction materials; raw materials needed for new buildings and roads. The highest rate of growth was observed for metallic raw materials; particularly iron, copper, and aluminum for the production of machines, vehicles, and electronics. (See also the website www.materialflows.net, which provides downloadable data on resource extraction.)

Using the concept of the so-called "Ecological Footprint" (see box "The Ecological Footprint"), it is possible to estimate whether the extent of people's current resource consumption

The Ecological Footprint

The Ecological Footprint illustrates how much land and water area is required for the long-term continuation of, for example, a city's or country's production and consumption. To calculate an Ecological Footprint, statistical data on human consumption in different categories (such as food, housing, transportation, etc.) is converted into bioproductive land areas. This allows us to calculate, for example, the amount of forest area needed (in the form of wood for making paper) to secure one person's annual paper consumption. The Ecological Footprint also includes the biologically productive area needed to absorb waste and emissions. A large portion of this area consists of forests which are necessary to assimilate carbon dioxide, released into the atmosphere when fossil fuels are combusted, in the form of biomass. This concept can also help us to estimate how much biologically productive land and water area is available in a particular country, or on the Earth as a whole. A comparison of an area's Ecological Footprint with the existent biological capacity tells us whether humanity still has an ecological surplus, and room for further growth, or is already overusing natural systems.

already exceeds Earth's long-term ecological capacity. Such estimates confirm that today the human race is already living at a level that overshoots Earth's regenerative capacity by approximately one-fifth. The conservation organization WWF, together with other organizations, publishes a bi-annual report on this topic, the last appeared in 2006. If we want to continue extracting raw materials and quenching our thirst for energy without damaging our planet's ecosystem, then we would already need more than one Earth! Put another way: humankind has already begun to withdraw the "principal" of the natural capital available on our planet instead of living off the "interest."

Modern cities' hunger for resources

Large modern cities provide a good example for the dependency of human activities upon nature, as a city cannot function without the constant input of raw materials and energy. Every urban area needs a natural hinterland. The hinterland begins at the city limits; where fruit, vegetables, and grain are cultivated, and gravel and sand are excavated as construction material for houses and roads. And it ends on other continents; where, for example, crude oil or natural gas is extracted for energy supply, and metallic raw materials (such as iron ore or copper) are mined. In many areas of the world, agriculture is correspondingly intensive. Even though, on a global scale, fewer and fewer people live in rural areas, the natural systems of these areas are used ever more intensively to provide cities with natural resources. At the same time, mining is increasing in many African and Latin American regions. The mining products serve as raw materials for secondary products of a higher value, such as cars or computers, which are then sold in the cities. Therefore, no city can achieve sustainability autonomously.

More and more people are leaving rural areas for the cities. For the first time in human history more than 50% of the global population now lives in urban areas. According to UN prognoses, by the year 2030 this number will have swelled to two-thirds; of this growth, 90% will take place in so-called developing countries (for more information, see: http://www.unfpa.org/pds/urbaniza-tion.htm). Consequently, in the future, cities will have even more responsibility for ensuring that natural systems are handled in an environmentally-friendly manner. In the globalized world, cities will increasingly become the hubs of exchange and consumption of natural resources. At the same time, with respect to securing their supply, large cities will become vulnerable, because they are dependent upon energy, food, and water that often come from areas far away.

As an example, let's take a look at two large German cities: Berlin (calculated by Schnauss in 2001) and Hamburg (calcu-lated by Jancke in 1999); in both cases, resource consumption was measured using the Ecological Footprint (compare box "The Ecological Footprint"). The results of the calculations show that a Berliner's Ecological Footprint is around 4.4 hectares annu-ally. This means that providing all natural resources necessary to satisfy the consumption needs of a person living in Berlin requires on average an area of 4.4 hectares per year, or more than six soccer fields. For the entire population of Berlin taken together, the area is thus more than fifteen million hectares. If we draw a circle of this size around Berlin, cities such as Rostock, Dresden, and Braunschweig would be within the circle, and its perimeter would even almost reach Hamburg! This calculation makes it clear just how large a city's ecological hinterland is. Hamburg's Ecological Footprint per capita is even larger; almost 5.5 hectares per person. There are two reasons for this difference: Firstly, the density of buildings in Berlin is higher; more people live on one square kilometer of urban area. Higher building density and fewer single-family homes also means lower consump-tion of energy, particularly for heating and transportation, and therefore a smaller Ecological Footprint. The second important difference is the average income: inhabitants of Hamburg are, on average, much more affluent than inhabitants of Berlin. More income also means more consumption, larger dwellings, faster cars, more long-distance travel – all of this causes the Footprint to grow.

If we add up all the Footprints of German cities, the sum is an area much larger than the total area of Germany. This clearly demonstrates that rich countries consume a significant portion of their Environmental Space in other regions of the world.

The rich against the poor: unequal distribution of natural resource use

People in different regions of the world, with different lifestyles, use up very different amounts of nature to satisfy their needs. The level of environmental consumption is determined mostly by a society's wealth; those with more money in their pockets also end up consuming more, as we have already seen in the comparison of Hamburg and Berlin.

The enormous differences in consumption can be plainly seen in a comparison of carbon dioxide emissions. Each inhabitant of Earth is responsible for approximately four metric tons of carbon dioxide emissions into the atmosphere per year (see Fig. 3.3). Climate researchers have calculated that a global reduction of at least 50% is necessary to stop climate change; see also Mojib Latif's book in this series. If one also makes allowances for population growth, the sustainable emissions level would be approximately 1.7 metric tons of carbon dioxide annually – the maximum amount each person would be allowed to produce per year. We only need to look at the current emissions of industrialized countries to see how far away from this goal we currently are. An American citizen produces on average almost twenty

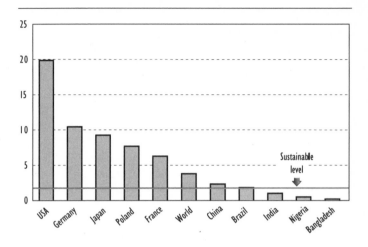

Figure 3.3 Per capita annual carbon dioxide emissions in ten selected countries

metric tons of carbon dioxide, the average European still produces eight metric tons. In contrast, per capita emissions in the developing countries are still below the sustainable level. This means that these countries may still raise their energy consumption and their carbon dioxide emissions in order to improve their citizens' standard of living, but the rich countries must lower their emissions considerably.

If we look at other natural resources, the picture is similar. The industrialized countries overuse the global Environmental Space, leaving little for the rest of the world, whereby an increasing portion of this Environmental Space lies outside the rich countries' borders. For example, in 2002, according to the World Resources Institute, every American used an average of 307 kilograms of paper and paper products; every German used

Global Environmental Space

The concept of Environmental Space is based on two principles. The environmental principle states that Earth can only withstand environmental burdens to a certain extent before our global ecosystems reach tipping points. If we want to grant future generations the same development opportunities we ourselves have had, without overusing nature, then we need to drastically reduce our use of natural resources. The second principle could be called the justice principle: Every person has in principle the same right to use Earth's natural resources.

By linking these two principles we can estimate how many resources are available for each inhabitant of our planet. Our Environmental Space therefore describes the total amount of energy, non-renewable raw materials, agricultural land, forests, etc. that each person may utilize without causing irreversible damage to natural systems.

The implementation of this concept presents an enormous challenge, particularly for the rich industrialized countries. They are the ones who consume the bulk of the global Environmental Space and accordingly are those who must cut back their consumption drastically.

219 kilograms; the Chinese, with a consumption of thirty-four kilograms, were far below the world average of fifty-two kilograms – although the trend is upwards. At the same time, the per capita consumption of the people in the poorest countries of the world, for example in Africa, is less than one kilogram. As we

Ecological rucksacks

When we buy a product, such as a kilogram of beef or a computer, the weight of this product is many times lower than the total amount of natural resources needed to produce it in the course of the production process. Ecological rucksacks (see Schmidt-Bleek, 2004) allow us to visualize the consumption of natural resources hidden behind every product or service.

Ecological rucksacks contain, on the one hand, those materials which need to be taken from nature in order to gain access to other, valuable, raw materials, although they themselves have no economic value and therefore also no price. They include, for example, overburden (rock and soil) removed when mining coal or ores. Even if these materials do not flow into the economy, they often have a negative impact on the environment; for example overburden contains acidic substances that are washed out and then drain into the groundwater.

On the other hand, ecological rucksacks illustrate the interlinked networks of international resource flows, because they also contain all those materials used in other countries to produce imported products (so-called upstream material requirements). These include, for example, the vast amounts of feed and water consumed by livestock bred for the export of meat and meat products to other countries. Or all the raw materials and energy needed to produce a computer imported from Japan or China. The weight of these ecological rucksacks is usually much higher than that of the imported good itself, and therefore reflects the environmental burden that the local consumption of products places on other countries.

can see, there is a huge difference between the poorest and the richest people of this world.

If we take the sum of all the raw materials and products that we consume in one year, we can determine the total material consumption per capita. Here, too, there are significant differences between the inhabitants of industrialized and developing countries, but the pattern is the same: the lowest consumption is in the poorest countries of Africa and South Asia. In these regions, per capita consumption is sometimes less than two metric tons annually. On the other end of the scale are the countries in Europe or the United States that have a consumption of fifteen to thirty-five metric tons per year. If we add the so-called ecological rucksacks (see box "Ecological rucksack"), we even arrive at amounts between forty and eighty metric tons annually for inhabitants of industrialized countries.

Global resource consumption in the future

The current overuse of our planet is even more dramatic when we consider the depth of material poverty with which a large portion of the world's population still must contend. If we take into account that the poorest countries' economies in particular must grow in order to at least secure the basic needs of their population for food, health, and housing to a greater extent than they do today, it becomes clear that the topic of environmental consumption is closely connected to the topic of global justice.

Estimates of the development of worldwide resource use over the next fifteen years show that global environmental consumption will increase dramatically if we continue to deal with nature as ruthlessly as we have to date. For example, it is predicted that the world-wide extraction of natural resources will swell to over eighty billion metric tons annually by 2020. This means a rise of over 40% in comparison to 2005, or a doubling in only forty years. Although it is the rich industrialized countries that have the highest per capita consumption by far, in the decades to come, other regions of the world (particularly East Asia, but also Latin America) will quickly catch up in their development. In the future, countries such as China, India, or Brazil (see below) will be responsible for a much larger portion of global resource consumption.

Concurrent with this rise in the use of the environment, there will also be a dramatic increase in the emission of greenhouse gases. Model calculations project a rise of global carbon dioxide emissions from currently around twenty-six billion metric tons to around thirty-five billion metric tons annually by 2020 – with expected negative impacts on our climate.

Humans are already causing irreversible natural damage by the way we manage our economy; this results in a central problem, particularly for the development of poor countries. The industrialized countries' economic model has been based on accumulating wealth first and taking care of environmental damage later. In our current situation, this path to development is no longer sustainable. Not only is it very expensive, it also ignores the ecological limits of our planet. In the past 300 years, today's industrialized nations have used a disproportional amount of global environmental resources in order to accumulate their wealth. If the developing countries now also take this path without radical changes in the means of production and in lifestyle, particularly in the rich countries, the world will inevitably head towards conflicts around social and environmental issues. If all the people of Earth consumed as much of the environment as the people of Europe, humanity would need almost three Earths to provide the necessary raw materials and energy.

In light of these prospects, the efficient use of material, energy, and land becomes ever more important. We now examine this aspect in more detail.

How efficiently do we use natural resources?

The developments observed worldwide over the past decades could be a cause for celebration: our economies are using raw materials and energy more and more efficiently. Therefore, in relative terms, less and less materials and energy are needed to produce one unit of economic output (one euro or dollar). The economy is therefore growing faster than the use of resources – put another way: economic growth and increased resource consumption have been "decoupled."

On the global level, approximately 25 % less raw materials were needed in 2002, compared to 1980, to make one dollar of value added; the material intensity of the global economy fell from a bit more than two kilograms per US dollar in 1980 to around 1.5 kilograms per US dollar in 2002 (see Behrens and colleagues, 2007). This reduction is due to new environmentally-friendly technologies used in more and more countries which use raw materials and energy more efficiently than the technology of twenty years ago. On the other hand, more and more economic wealth is accrued in services (banking, insurance, tourism, etc.). As a rule – to which there are of course exceptions: air travel for example uses an enormous amount of the environment – services have a lower environmental consumption than mining, agriculture, and industry. Overall, global economic production is therefore more efficient.

Nevertheless, there is no reason to relax our efforts: this increase in efficiency has not relieved the world's ecosystems, because at the same time humankind is producing more and more goods. Improvements in efficiency have been more than compensated by the ever larger amounts of goods produced. Whereas material intensity sank by 25%, the gross domestic product (GDP) of the global economy rose by no less than 83% between 1980 and 2002! This resulted in the absolute increase already described above.

A similar development can be seen in Europe, with the difference that there was no noticeable increase in the average European's resource use over the past twenty years; rather, it has remained stable at a high level. However, in Europe as well, there has been no reduction of material and energy consumption in this time period, because relative gains in efficiency have been canceled out by the growth of production and consumption.

These developments are also known under the term *rebound effect*: Improved material and energy efficiency lowers the costs of production, this enables industry to lower their market price. Consumers spend the money they have saved by buying cheaper products or other products; they buy more of these products, or replace them more often. Typical examples from the immediate past are computers or cell phones.

From the point of view of sustainable development, the main challenge for the economy is to satisfy the desire for increased affluence without a further increase in the consumption of natural resources. What is more, the general goal must be an absolute decoupling of economic activities and resource use and the concrete reduction of the latter. In the end, the absolute amount of resource use determines whether we overuse our planet's ecosystems or are able to reverse the trend and move towards sustainability. In other words, we must "dematerialize" our economy. As Friedrich Schmidt-Bleek has calculated, not just a small improvement, but a radical dematerialization by a factor of ten is necessary to realize this change.

The driving forces of current developments

A simple question arises here: Why is the increase in global resource consumption seemingly inexorable, what are the driving forces behind this trend? Four circumstances are responsible:

1. Nature is undervalued in our economy. Consequently, prices for energy and raw materials do not reflect the true ecological costs. Let us examine a typical production chain in the age of globalization: the manufacture of a car. The production chain begins with the extraction of raw materials, for example iron ore mined in Brazil. This iron ore is delivered to a steel mill in South Korea, which turns the iron into steel. The steel is bought by a Japanese car manufacturer and made into car bodies. Finally, the Japanese car is exported to Europe.

The value of each component of the car grows at each step of this production chain, because people, through their know-how, add value to the product. This added value determines a large portion of the price we pay the car retailer.

But which role do raw materials, energy, and water play – all those natural resources needed to manufacture the car? The fact that economic added value refers solely to the input by humans to a product has an enormous effect on the way we handle nature. Nature itself, which provides the foundation for every production process, is not taken into account in this calculation. This is because the raw materials, energy, and water we take from the earth have, in and of themselves, no price in our economic system.

The objection that there are commodities markets on which natural goods – from grain and pork to oil and gold – are traded, often at high prices, is irrelevant. Here, too, the prices for these products are determined only by economic factors: How much does it cost to extract the above-mentioned iron ore from the Earth? This asks only about costs for machines, miners, etc. Furthermore, prices on the commodities markets are also governed by the laws of supply and demand. High demand and low supply bring a high price – as can currently be seen very well in the case of oil or steel.

In all instances, our economic system deals only with those values created by humans and added to nature, but never with the value nature's services themselves have for us (Porritt, 2005). This way of looking at things is an important reason for our wasteful dealings with nature.

Another example also shows that the current calculation of a country's economic performance makes a false assessment of the factor nature. From an economic viewpoint, it's entirely positive when nature is damaged and the economy is called upon to make an attempt to reinstate the original state. For example, when an oil tanker runs aground and thousands of tons of oil spill into the sea and are washed ashore, it brings a growth spurt for the economy. Special units of environmental technicians must rush to the scene to apply chemicals to the oil in the water to decontaminate it, or to dig out and transport contaminated sand. Pollution creates a demand for certain services, which boosts economic growth. At the same time, the planet's losses, the thousands of fish and birds who die as a result of the accident, are not added into the economic calculation – unless farm animals are lost.

Nature either has no price or much too low a price to send a signal to product manufacturers and consumers that we need to treat her better. One central goal of environmental and sustainability policy must therefore be to create a framework which makes polluters financially liable for the environmental damage they cause.

2. Another fundamental reason for constant growth is the fact that our money and profit-centered economy focuses primarily on one goal: turning a sum of money into a greater sum of money. This is the main reason why companies produce goods at all: to make a profit. And private investors, too, are always searching for the highest possible returns on their savings.

However, to be able to invest, companies must usually take out loans which they later must pay back (to banks or investment funds for example) with interest. For a company to be successful, it is therefore not enough for the sale of its products (or services) to cover all costs of production (for example the input of machines and labor) and leave a profit margin. It must also generate enough income to be able to pay back the interest on its loans. And additional income can only be made by selling more products. Interest, therefore, forces companies to continually produce more, that is, to grow.

The economy grows, and with it the amount of disposable income. Ever larger sums of this money are put into savings or invested, for example in pension plans. For every 100 euros of disposable income in Germany in 2005, more than eleven euros went into savings. Today, the sum total of money saved in Germany, as reported by Deutsche Postbank, amounts to no less than 155 billion euros! Whenever more money is saved, at the same time there must be more debtors (companies, private households, or the government) who pick up this monetary surplus in the form of loans in order to invest it or spend it on consumption. This is the only way the economic and monetary cycles can come full circle. This is also the cycle of the growth spiral driven by this monetary system: more growth – more money – more loans – more interest due – more production and consumption – more growth.

The obligation to pay interest also has an important

international dimension. Since the 1970s, developing countries have increasingly taken out loans and become indebted to industrialized countries. Developing country debt is continuously growing and has today already risen to astronomic heights: Based on World Bank data, the German development aid organization Welthungerhilfe has calculated a rise from around 1,300 billion US dollars in 1990 to 2,500 billion US dollars in 2004. In many developing countries, the debt is higher than the total annual national income. Many countries, particularly in Latin America, have to use more than a quarter of their export revenues to pay back their debts. And since many developing countries specialize in the extraction and export of raw materials (see below), rising debt leads directly to the increased exploitation of nature: more crude oil production, more mines for the extraction of metallic raw materials, faster clear-cutting of rainforests for tropical woods and to create cropland and pastures.

Cancellation of debt, particularly for the poorest countries, is therefore not only an important measure in the fight against poverty, but can also ease the pressure on the natural resources of these countries and thus also contribute to the protection of our planet's ecosystems.

3. The level of the current global consumption of nature is, as explained above, primarily determined by the industrialized nations, whose inhabitants have by far the highest per capita consumption of energy and raw materials. However, this is going to change. In the coming decades, especially aspiring industrialized countries in Asia (principally China and India, but also countries such as Indonesia and Malaysia) and in Latin America (Brazil, Argentina, Mexico) will catch up regarding resource use, increasing global consumption even more.

In the past ten to fifteen years, the above-named countries

have strongly promoted their industrialization process, economic growth rates of 6 to 10% annually were not uncommon – a development which would be the envy of every European economic policy-maker.

Concurrent with this economic growth, the demand for raw materials, energy, and land area has risen sharply. In 2004, China alone, for example, already consumed 7% of the oil produced globally, 30% of the iron ore, 31% of the coal, one-quarter of the aluminum, and 27% of all steel products – and the trend is a continuing steep increase (Blume, 2004). The result of the economic upturn: in all of the above-named countries, this economic upswing is currently giving rise to a new class of consumers who increasingly model their lifestyle on the West – including all the products which also are a part of our daily life: cars, televisions, washers, notebooks, cell phones. The sociologist Wolfgang Sachs of the Wuppertal Institute coined the term "transnational consumer class" for this phenomenon (see Wuppertal Institute, 2005). He thus expresses the fact that the lifestyles of the upper classes of Rio de Janeiro, Cape Town, and Beijing have more in common with one another than with the lifestyles of people from different social classes within the same cities.

Growth in these new consumer nations will cause a further sharp rise in the use of renewable and non-renewable resources in the coming decades. Gravel, sand, and cement will be required for new buildings in the fast-growing cities; fossil fuels (particularly coal and crude oil) for meeting the energy needs of industry and private homes; metallic raw materials for machines and consumer goods; and cellulose for the mounting demand for paper.

However, negative environmental impacts are already so obvious that Pan Yue, Deputy Director of the Chinese State Environmental Protection Administration, has sounded the alarm. One-third of Chinese cities suffer from excessive air pollution, one-third of Chinese land area is threatened by desertification, one-third of rural rivers and no less than 90% of rivers which run through Chinese cities are severely polluted. Environmental problems in China are already enormous – also in regard to economic costs. According to recent estimates of the World Bank and the Chinese Academy of Sciences, annual environmental damage accounts for at least 8% and perhaps even 15% of the Chinese Gross Domestic Product (GDP). In plain language, this means that in the long term, environmental damage and resource losses will cancel out economic success. Politicians such as the Chinese Deputy Director of the Environmental Protection Administration cited above now advocate a new kind of growth oriented towards qualitative rather than quantitative goals. China, with its 1.3 billion people, cannot afford to get rich first and repair environmental damage later – following the path of the industrialized countries. The environmental damage, as the Deputy Director said, will have destroyed the foundations of the Chinese economy before China can become rich.

4. A further important reason for the increase in global resource consumption is the international trade in goods between countries on different continents, which has expanded dramatically in the past decades. Never before have so many products been exchanged between the large economic blocs of Europe, the USA, and Japan. The above-mentioned upward climbers in Asia and Latin America are also increasingly being woven into the net of worldwide trade. The main reasons for these developments are on the one hand falling tariffs and trade barriers, forced through by the World Trade Organization (WTO) in particular with the goal of facilitating the exchange of goods. On the other hand, transporting raw materials and goods around the globe is only profitable because fossil fuels, particularly oil, are still cheap in

comparison to other factors such as labor. This is due to the fact that the consequential costs of fossil fuels, the consumption of nature, are not reflected in the price of oil. This situation has led to an almost explosive rise in world trade in the last fifty years – the world has become our supermarket. If we add up the value of the exports of all countries – the WTO publishes annual statistics on international trade – world trade has expanded in this time period no less than ninety-fold! No wonder that globalization is a highly controversial topic.

Supporters of the further increase in international trade such as the WTO or the World Bank argue that more trade leads to more economic growth. This would have positive economic effects, such as more efficiency and falling production costs in companies. For in a globalized world, companies can produce where it is cheapest and the highest profit can be realized. Although this policy holds clear advantages for companies, it increases the pressure on European governments to dismantle social achievements (such as the forty-hour work week) and environmental standards (such as the strict regulation of air pollution). The argument is that this is the only strategy available if they are to remain competitive internationally and prevent even more companies from moving to countries with cheaper labor, worse working conditions, and less environmental regulation.

Supporters of globalization also contend that more trade leads to an improvement of environmental conditions. Only more growth can give national governments the opportunity to levy higher taxes and pay more for environmental protection, they argue. Furthermore, developing countries will also change their economic structures as a result of economic growth. They would no longer primarily supply raw materials and carry out simple manufacturing tasks for the industrialized nations, but would change their economies and provide more environmentally-friendly services like those which are established today in the rich countries.

Critics of a further intensification of international trade counter that it has been exactly the steady growth of trade on the global market that has led to an ever greater use of natural resources. From this perspective, world trade is not a solution, but one of the main causes of increasing resource use and the spread of pollution on the global level. Technical progress today allows people to exploit even less accessible resource deposits faster and faster and at continuously falling costs. Added to this are factors such as quicker monetary transfers, more reliable international legal agreements, better systems of communication, and higher transportation capacity; these all speed up the development of international trade.

At the same time, the social tensions which are part and parcel of this dynamic development are becoming increasingly apparent. The integration of more and more countries into the global economy described above does not lead to the equal distribution of progress throughout every country. On the contrary, globalization exacerbates differences between different regions; some cities, such as Shanghai or Bombay, are booming, while at the same time people in rural areas remain poor or are even becoming poorer.

From the viewpoint of environmental sustainability, there is another pivotal point: In the age of global markets, every consumer who has enough income at his or her disposal can satisfy his or her need for the consumption of natural goods by buying products from throughout the world: bananas from Costa Rica, apples from Chile, pineapples from South Africa, wine from Australia, a laptop from Taiwan, and a new car from South Korea. Because of globalization, every local natural resource is subject to the highest possible demand, namely the demand of transnational producers and consumers on the world markets. Traditional regional limitations of material consumption are increasingly being lost in today's world. The consequence is that more and more countries are exploiting natural resources to an extent far above the ecological capacity of their own country. They are accumulating so-called "ecological deficits."

When a country's economy produces an ecological deficit, this means it is either living at the expense of generations to come, because it is destroying the natural resources which are the foundation of its society, or it is living at the expense of other countries. Globalization also leads to a redistribution of environmental consumption on the one hand and negative impacts for the environment and for humans on the other.

Global resource justice

Redistributing environmental burdens

Due to the increasingly interwoven nature of the global economy, we must examine the topics of resource availability and resource justice on the global level. In the past twenty years, many industrial countries have progressively relocated their resource supply to other areas of the world. To an ever greater extent, the local extraction of raw materials has been reduced and replaced by imports from other regions of the world. This has increased many industrialized countries' dependency on foreign suppliers, in particular regarding fossil fuels and metallic raw materials.

In the member states of the European Union, for example, there has been a trend since the 1990s towards a clear reduction in the movement of materials connected to, in particular, coal mining and the extraction of minerals. During the same period, the ecological rucksacks of imports grew. Increasingly, environmental impacts are being outsourced to other parts of the world, concurrent with the mining and processing of raw materials (see Schütz and colleagues, 2004). In this way, due to the system of international trade, Europe can improve environmental quality within its own borders and relocate the environmental impacts caused by our consumption habits to other regions of the world.

Industrialized areas such as Europe, however, can import and use more and more resources only if other regions increasingly act as resource suppliers. And in fact, in the past twenty years, many so-called developing countries have become more specialized than ever before in the extraction and export of raw materials and environmentally intensive products. Soy and iron ore from Brazil, copper and gold from Chile and Peru, bananas from Ecuador and the Philippines, oil from Nigeria and Venezuela – the list could go on almost indefinitely. In these regions, increased extraction of raw materials causes intensifying environmental problems, such as the destruction of fertile soil due to mining, clear-cutting rain forests to make room for plantations or pastures, or water and air pollution, from which the local population suffers most. The way in which poor countries are integrated into the world market has led to a global redistribution of environmental impact. The overuse of resources by Europe and other industrialized regions is directly connected to topics such as poverty and justice.

This division of the world into regions that extract resources, others that process them, and yet others that consume the final product has dire consequences for the distribution of economic success and prosperity. The rich countries manage to position themselves well on the world markets: relatively cheap raw materials (for example, steel) are imported on the whole from poor regions of the world or from emerging economies, processed in Europe (for example, incorporated into a machine), and finally exported again with a much higher economic value. Profits from the international exchange of goods are therefore made mostly in the rich countries.

In this system, developing countries fall into an economic trap: they become more and more dependent upon the export of only a few products (mostly raw materials such as coffee, soy, metals, etc.). At the same time, the prices for the sale of these products have fallen sharply between the 1950s and the end of the last century. Therefore, many of these countries have only been able to maintain their level of income by exporting ever larger amounts of natural resources – and suffering all the negative environmental impact that accompanies the increased exploitation of nature. However, at this point we must mention that, mostly because of the dramatic rise in resource consumption on the part of fast-growing threshold countries such as China and India, the trend towards falling prices for raw materials has been reversed. On the one hand, this development, at least in the short term, has improved the economic situation of countries that export raw materials. On the other hand, conditions have gotten worse for poor developing countries that, for example, are dependent upon the import of food.

In other words, it can be argued that globalization promotes the polarization of the world: on one side are the "economies of processing," especially the industrialized countries and the economically successful regions of the developing world, which benefit from globalization, and on the other side are the "economies of poverty," the poor and poorest countries of the world, which are emerging as the losers of globalization.

Less consumption and more just distribution

If the above is true, sustainable development in a limited Environmental Space can be achieved only if two conditions are met.

Firstly, humankind must live within the limits of the Earth's ecological capacity to prevent the further exacerbation of global environmental problems, so that our children and grandchildren do not inherit a damaged ecosphere. Since we have already overshot the Earth's ecological capacity, at least in some areas, we (particularly the wealthy portion of the global population) must reduce our use of nature (contraction). Secondly, natural resources must be distributed more fairly between the inhabitants of different regions of the world. A world in which half of the population consumes excessive amounts while the other half goes hungry (or even starves) cannot be sustainable. It is just as important that countries and regions equalize their consumption levels (convergence) – on a level within the ecological capacity of the biosphere. The Contraction and Convergence model joins ecology and justice (see Fig. 3.4).

Within this framework, industrialized and developing countries take two different development paths towards the future.

The industrialized countries, as the countries with the highest consumption, must reduce their consumption and stop overusing Global Environmental Space. Only then will there be enough ecological surplus for developing countries to increase their material prosperity. This climb must not, however, result in permanent growth of natural resource consumption; after a time, it must meet the level of the industrialized countries at a sustainable level.

At the same time, developing countries must increase their efforts at slowing down population growth, as we have seen in Chapter 1. Per capita savings will not help if the number of people continues to swell as quickly as it has in the past decades.

Another important key to sustainability for both industrialized and developing countries alike is resource productivity. This means, as vividly described by Friedrich Schmidt-Bleek in his

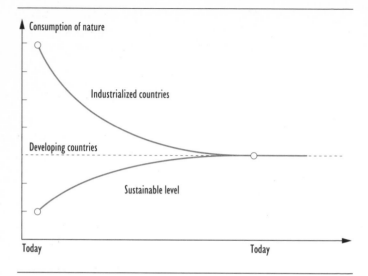

Figure 3.4 Contraction and convergence

book *The Earth: Natural Resources and Human Intervention*, nothing less than a new Industrial Revolution devoted to the dramatic improvement of resource productivity.

What this economy of the future could look like is the subject of Chapter 4.

4 Visions of a Sustainable Future

In the preceding chapters, we put forward the challenges that the world's societies are facing. They must be met differently in the "North" and in the "South," but the overriding goal is just and sustainable development – meaning the responsible use of natural capital and closing the gap between "poor" and "rich." If we are to achieve sustainable development, we must drastically reduce resource consumption, particularly in those areas where the global consumer class is concentrated (North America, Europe, and Japan); allowing poorer areas of the world to catch up without themselves "overusing" nature. It is a matter of the just distribution of resource use.

That's why we would like to begin this chapter with a vision. A vision is an ideal picture of the future – in Europe and in the whole world. Every company, every individual needs a vision and the goals derived from it in order to be able to work and live happily.

Our vision is an ongoing, adaptable societal process which leads the world down the path towards sustainability. But won't this mean giving up so much that is near and dear to us in life? Don't we have to choose between less prosperity and an environmentally-friendly economy, or economic growth and the concurrent destruction of our planet? In our vision, we will drastically reduce the speed of global environmental changes without forgoing the good life; at the same time distributing prosperity more fairly.

This vision rests on two pillars: *efficiency* and *sufficiency*. On the one hand, it is possible to produce almost all goods and services that make our life pleasant while consuming a great deal less material, energy, and land area; thereby appreciably reducing ecological footprints and rucksacks. This is the pillar of improved *ecological efficiency*. On the other hand, it is becoming increasingly clear that the accumulation of material wealth contributes less and less to the good life for all those people who have reached a certain level of prosperity. The question must be asked whether it might be possible for us to dispense with a further increase in our supply of goods and still be able to live ever better. This pillar is the *sufficiency* strategy. These two strategies complement one another and, in the end, merge into *one* sustainable development.

The efficiency strategy

How can the economy help achieve a sustainable future? Firstly, the production and consumption of goods and services are responsible for global environmental change. Secondly, the economy also produces our prosperity. It therefore stands to reason that the economy is the central starting point for the efficiency strategy.

Nature pays for every good produced by human hands because natural resources are consumed during its manufacture, use, and disposal. The modern service society is also characterized by diverse, complicated technologies whose interaction must function perfectly around the clock. This is true of a train ride, of getting money from an automated teller machine, or of reading a bedtime story to your grandchild.

In general, the rule is: the less input of natural resources, the more eco-intelligently a society functions. However, societies will only then be sustainable with respect to material when we have left the current extremely material-intensive lifestyle of the industrialized world behind us. Without a dramatic rise in resource productivity, a sustainable economy and sustainable economic growth cannot be achieved. The principle of 'eco-efficiency' must become the benchmark of our economy.

The question is whether we will be able to satisfy our "needs" eco-intelligently in the future. The first step is as exact a definition as possible of what we really want and need (this, among other things, is the focus of the German-American philosopher Fritjhof Bergmann). The next step is to search for ways to fulfill our needs by technical means that use as few natural resources as possible; including material, energy, and land area – and this from the "cradle to the grave" (see box "Eco-efficiency"). It goes without saying that in doing so the usual technical, physical, and chemical regulations for production must be adhered to and that we must also make use of tried and true technologies and manufacturing processes.

Diverse technical and societal innovations are necessary to achieve eco-efficient production. In terms of resource input, we need to improve the resource efficiency of the technologies we use today, and we need new consumer goods and new production processes. Economists speak of product and process innovation.

When the term "rationalization" is mentioned, most companies think of reducing labor costs. Reducing the costs for the materials used in the production process, which are often considerable, is usually ignored. Nevertheless, the more efficient use of the technologies implemented today is relatively easy to achieve. Company controllers focus primarily on the labor factor, because in the past salaries rose continuously whereas prices for

Eco-efficiency – from the cradle to the grave

The term "eco-efficiency" was coined around fifteen years ago to show ways in which our economy can produce more value added with less input. The Swiss entrepreneur Stephan Schmidheiny, founder of the World Business Council for Sustainable Development, popularized the term in his book *Changing Course*, published in 1992 on the occasion of the UN Conference on Environment and Development in Rio. Some years later, Ernst Ulrich von Weizsäcker and colleagues introduced a simple formula for eco-efficiency in the book *Factor Four: Doubling Wealth – Halving Resource Use*.

In his books, Friedrich Schmidt-Bleek often reiterates the fact that one must look at resource consumption "system-wide" in order to obtain correct eco-efficiency data: not only a product's use (for example a car's gas mileage) must be taken into account, but everything natural that is used, from the resources extracted for the product to the final and environmentally sound disposal of the product (thus "from the cradle to the grave" of the product at hand). The sum of this "material input" should be utilized as intensively as possible, meaning distributed over as many units of use as possible, according to Schmidt-Bleek. The "material intensity per unit of service" (MIPS for short) must be kept as low as possible.

raw materials may have been subject to great fluctuations, but they followed no clear tendency. Because of this, there is often simply a lack of knowledge about resource-saving alternatives to conventional production processes.

Business consultants report that even providing nothing more than technical advice on such alternatives for companies in the processing sector could bring savings of around 20% of material costs (see Fischer et al., 2004). In a study for the Aachen Foundation, it was shown that considerable outcomes could be achieved if, over the course of twelve years, an information campaign on improving resource efficiency were able to reach all companies in the processing sector in Germany. Clearly, falling material consumption also goes hand in hand with economic success: costs for consultation and information are incurred only once, whereas production becomes more efficient for good with respect to material consumption. During the course of the information campaign, the gross domestic product would rise by approximately 1% annually. Nevertheless, resource consumption and economic growth would be decoupled, and resource use would remain at today's level. The number of employees would rise by around one million, and the government would profit from a long-lasting improvement in its budget situation. A detailed account of this and similar studies (in German) can be found in the Aachen Foundation's report.

In Germany, the Hannover Chamber of Commerce, for example, determined that materials currently account for 40% of the costs in manufacturing industries – as compared to labor, which accounts for 23% (Fig. 4.1). One reason for the usual miscalculation of the true proportion of costs lies in accounting systems that often record labor costs as separate items on diverse accounts, whereas material costs are aggregated, usually in just a single account, without differentiating

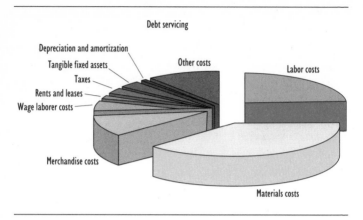

Figure 4.1 Cost structure of the manufacturing industry

between individual groups of materials. It is thus impossible to calculate the real consumption of individual materials and their exact share of the cost of the product. The International Federation of Accountants, the umbrella organization for company controllers and tax accountants, recently pointed this out in its new *Guidance for Environmental Management Accounting*, which explicitly recommends counting losses of materials in order to assess environment-related costs (see Jasch and Savage, 2005).

Indeed, more and more companies are recognizing the advantages of saving resources: companies, customers, and the environment benefit from increased efficiency in the use of raw materials, supplies, and primary products. Costs decrease, competitiveness increases, and the diminished input of raw materials as well as less waste relieves the environment.

Technology can make an important contribution to this goal because new technologies make increased resource productivity possible. Companies can increase their material efficiency at several points:

- Product design (smaller products with a longer life-span and more uses)
- Management processes (for example, systematically controlling resource consumption)
- Service orientation instead of product orientation (see the following examples).

Two examples demonstrate the changes to which we are aspiring: If we could manage in the future to produce textiles that hardly needed to be cleaned because they repel dirt and odors, enormous amounts of water, solvents, and detergent could be saved. In the information technology sector, innovative chips with higher resource productivity would also generate huge savings.

We need to think systemically to help find truly innovative solutions. For example, a "three-liter car" says nothing about the eco-efficiency of the product, for it is possible that the consumption of natural resources per person-kilometer (from production to use and environmentally sound disposal) is higher than that of a competing product which perhaps consumes five liters of gasoline per hundred kilometers. And trading in a washer that still works for a new one that uses less electricity can be the wrong decision from an environmental point of view if more energy and raw materials are used in the production of the new washer than the old one needs for its "life-cycle."

Examples of material-efficient production

The following are best practice examples of how companies have successfully implemented the principle of increased resource productivity (Friedrich Schmidt-Bleek gives more examples in his book in this series, *The Earth: Natural Resources and Human Intervention*).

Cooling with the heat of the sun

This seeming contradiction has been a challenge for inventors and engineers since the invention of solar collectors. Solitem GmbH has solved the problem and developed energy supply systems to cool buildings with the help of a solar-powered absorption chiller. This reduces emissions of pollutants and saves enormous amounts of energy (http://www.solitem.de).

Factor 100 in the paper industry

Process innovation has enabled a marked dematerialization of the industrial production of paper. Around the turn of the last century, approximately 500 to 1000 liters of water were needed to produce one kilogram of paper. Today, German paper factories use only six to twelve liters per kilogram of paper. Industrial water is now used in closed cycles; today, water circulates through the production process up to ten times – carefully filtered each time, of course. Energy consumption per kilogram of paper or cardboard has also fallen dramatically: by around 67% since 1955. However, the fact that the overall consumption of paper continues to rise also shows that we cannot be satisfied with product and process innovation alone; we need to think about further measures beyond pure product development and process design. The "paperless office" of the future was without a doubt one of the most serious false predictions of the late 20th century.

Not only can increased material efficiency in the production and use of individual products lower resource consumption; more service orientation can also help. A key insight on the path to higher resource productivity is that our quality of life depends primarily not on ownership of a product, but on its utility. In many cases, consumer needs are not focused on the product itself, but on its use; in other words on the service the product provides. We have to ask ourselves if it is truly necessary to own a car, a computer, or a drill ourselves, or whether there might be other ways of making use of these objects only at the times we actually need them. This approach opens up a variety of opportunities for saving materials.

Using rather than buying – for example, car sharing

Why own something you rarely use, when most of the time it just stands around taking up space and incurring costs? Many people don't drive their car every day. Getting together with others and using a product jointly in the form of *car sharing* raises utilization capacity and also saves money and the bother of buying and maintaining a car. This is also true for construction and agricultural machinery.

Warmth rather than heating – for example, energy contracting

The term "contracting" also means buying utility, rather than owning products. As an example: a company does not buy important machinery (for example heating and cooling systems, or even manufacturing equipment) and then own and operate it. Instead, a contractor installs and maintains the machinery and sells the service called for (for example a certain room temperature) to the client. In this way, machinery is used and operated more efficiently, the client has less system failures to contend with, and the maintenance and cost of the system are passed on to the contractor.

Selling utility and know-how – chemical leasing

In this case, business interests lie not in finding a market for chemicals, but in finding a market for the chemical services provided by the chemicals (for example, cleaning or varnishing). The basis of the business transaction is no longer the chemical compound, but the producer's and service provider's "chemical know-how." Here too, it is the utility that is sold, not the substance. The provider is no longer interested in selling as much of his product as possible; on the contrary, for the provider *and* the buyer, the service (for example painting a fender a certain color) is most economical when as little material (paint) as possible is used. The OECD, the association of industrialized countries, has recognized the importance of this field and recently organized a conference on this subject.

The innovative potential of market economies based on competition is enormous. In the past 200 years, the productivity of labor in the industrialized countries has soared. This process has in no way come to an end. Particularly in the processing industries, which are also at the center of discussions about resource consumption, many industries in Germany have experienced productivity increases of 5% per year and more; a process which, with much lower increases in production, leads to a constant decrease in the input of labor in this sector. Why shouldn't a similarly speedy process of innovation also be possible regarding resource input?

The unemployment problem, which currently causes great societal burdens in many countries, can be positively affected if an efficiency strategy is followed consistently and can perhaps even be solved completely. Technical progress is moving in the direction of saving materials and away from the goal of increasing labor productivity. We need to understand that raising prices of materials leads to an increase in material efficiency. In this case, two influences work together: the scarcities that can currently be observed on many commodities markets drive prices higher. At the same time, taxes and other charges also raise the prices of materials. This inevitably causes capital, as a factor of production created by the input of large amounts of material, to become more expensive, which in turn means that labor as a factor of production becomes cheaper in comparison. This lowers the incentive to replace labor with capital. Thus the dilemma of many affluent Western societies – that due to the fast growth rate of labor productivity, the employment situation can only be improved by an even higher growth rate in the production of goods – could finally have an end.

The sufficiency strategy

We have seen that they really do exist: the potentials to lower the use of resources substantially without a simultaneous reduction in our prosperity. However, what if the efficiency strategy alone does not lead to a substantial drop in resource consumption, emissions, and waste production; what if economic growth "eats up" the efficiency gains? To date, everything we have won via efficiency has been more than canceled out by the production of new goods and services (see Chapter 3). Sometimes it is even eco-efficiency measures themselves (*rebound effect*) that are responsible for this happening: more economic activity – more consumption of the environment. Money moves nature. This is true on a global level as well as for the European or the American economy.

If these misgivings prove to be true, then the growth in labor productivity cannot be substantially reduced by an increase in material efficiency, and unemployment will not disappear. If, however, environmental goals are not reached due to the rebound effect, and furthermore the social goal of increasing employment is not attained, then the goal of sustainability can only be met by explicitly renouncing economic growth.

An added factor is that, at the latest since the end of the boom of the "new economy" in the year 2000, the engine of Europe's economic growth machine has begun to stutter. Economic growth, which has brought so much material prosperity to those of us in the rich parts of the world for the past fifty years, seems to have relocated to other parts of the world. Nevertheless, the economies of the highly industrialized countries are today more productive than ever. As we have described, material prosperity can be created with less and less input of labor. This is the crux of the problem: To (re)instate full employment, many more goods and services would have to be produced and with them many more natural resources consumed. However, demand is "weak," and the economy is "limping along." People are buying less than needed to achieve "full employment." On the one hand, this is because they have less money in their pockets and believe their future will be even worse. And on the other hand, many people today already own a lot of things.

As we can see, we are dealing with two parallel developments: what is won by means of efficiency is more than compensated for by the production of new goods and services and, in addition, today already more people are consuming less – although there are a variety of reasons for this, not least rampant unemployment. Is turning away from an increase in the production of goods and services an alternative?

More affluence does not always mean more happiness

In the end, we must ask ourselves why we need to work so much and whether it wouldn't make more sense to distribute gainful employment among more people. However, working less would also mean less economic activity and thus less growth. Would this be a catastrophe? Not really – at least not if we accept something openly expressed by many economists: economic growth is *not* a measure for social progress. It is only what it is: the sum of everything that a country, region, or the whole world produced this year which exceeds the production of the previous year.

If that is so, then what is social progress? Generally speaking, it means that we are doing *better* each year – in a qualitative sense. This brings us back to the call for sustainable development. At its core, sustainable development means creating the conditions for preserving and improving quality of life for all people in the long term.

What we need to do is bring the goal of a good quality of life for all people, now and in the future, back to the foreground and decouple it from economic production. Only the goal of a better quality of life – protecting the environment and reducing poverty – can justify making changes, based on long-term and highly ethical principles.

For some years now, more and more writing in academic literature, but also in the mass media (from the *New York Times* to *Psychology Today* to *Stern* and *Brigitte* (German news and women's magazines)), has been providing well-founded analyses of what most people really want: a better quality of life as the basis for their individual happiness. Official documents, such as the EU Sustainable Development Strategy adopted in 2006, use the term *human well-being* to denote the measure of that which should be the goal of all policy. Since this field is developing rapidly, we refer here to the websites of the Austrian happiness research initiative (www.work-life-society-happiness.net), Karuna Consult (www.heartsopen.com), and the World Data Base of Happiness (www.eur.nl/fsw/happiness).

In Bhutan, a country in the Himalayas with a population of 635,000, the goal of a better quality of life became part of official government policy for the first time. King Jigme Singye Wangchuck says that gross national happiness is more important to him than gross national product. Gross national happiness is the guiding principle for planning and development in Bhutan. Much of the content of this concept has its roots in the age-old cultural heritage of Bhutan and its religious tradition of Buddhism. His Holiness the Dalai Lama has continually and succinctly stated: "All people want to be happy and free from suffering." Transcending suffering and striving towards happiness can be seen as the core of Buddhism. In Christianity as well, values such as loving your neighbor or protecting creation play a central role.

Obviously, happiness can not be enacted by law. Rather, the goal must be to create the political, cultural, and economic frameworks necessary for enabling people to develop and live out their individual happiness. The government of Bhutan tries to make this vision reality on four levels: by economic development, by the protection of culture and nature, and by good governance.

In contrast, international studies have shown that most people in the industrialized countries act to a large measure in a manner counter to their personal happiness and that of many other people. Work and consumption give them little (and at most very short-term) happiness, while many of their activities have very negative impacts on the environment and on other people, particularly in developing countries. Put another way: not only are the consumption and lifestyle of most people (keyword: "throw-away society") not sustainable; they also do little to

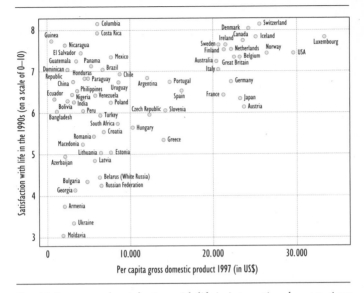

Figure 4.2 Income and satisfaction with life in international comparison

improve quality of life. Increasingly often there are discussions on material consumption being no more than an addiction able to provide only superficial compensation for deficits in "inner values": the desire for self-fulfillment, good relationships, and living in harmony with nature.

More and more people are realizing that the good life means more than always having new cars, vacations, clothing, sweets, or consumer electronics. Instead, they want relationships, relaxation, pleasure, and leisure. All of these goods *also* need material production – but it is not their most important precondition.

Of course, there is a correlation between prosperity and well-being. Figure 4.2 shows the connection between income and satisfaction in international comparison. There is a trend towards citizens of rich countries being happier than the inhabitants of countries with a lower per capita income. However, although there is a positive connection, it is not linear. Above an annual income of 20,000 US dollars, there is hardly any link between income and satisfaction with life.

Today's situation exhibits some similarities to the debate of the 1960s, when people noticed a discrepancy between "private wealth" and "public poverty." While the availability of consumer goods rose considerably after World War II for large segments of the population, the provision of public goods (schools, public transportation, culture, or also environmental protection) at first had to catch up; finally leading to the significant development of the "social welfare state" (in the broadest sense, including cultural and recreational institutions). In this case as well, material prosperity came before the need for social services.

Scientific research on happiness confirms the numbers given above: more consumption of products and services does not noticeably increase the well-being of those who, relatively, already own a lot. Increasingly, free time (time for relationships, for self-fulfillment, and for community involvement) also contributes to individual happiness.

Even if material prosperity and monetary income play only a limited role in determining individual well-being, there is nevertheless a very unequal distribution of human happiness, both within industrialized societies as well as between "North" and "South." The reason is poverty. Many people are unhappy because they are poor, while in the industrialized parts of the world many people are unhappy *although* they are rich. "Happiness for all and for always" is, however, part of the definition of sustainable development. This way of putting it makes it stand to reason that there is a relationship between my "happiness" and the "unhappiness" of others, who are not even able to satisfy their basic needs (for food, health, housing, etc.). From a sustainable development perspective, those who own more therefore have a responsibility to ensure a more just distribution of income, satisfying work, and at the very least a basic level of material prosperity for poor people.

This is not only true for the difference between the industrialized world (Europe, North America, Japan, and Australia) and the developing countries. Within the industrialized countries as well, the gap between "rich" and "poor" is becoming ever larger, so that we must also question the distribution of prosperity within our society – particularly the distribution of paid labor and income.

The old concepts of economic growth and comprehensive social welfare no longer seem to work. All that they do is redistribute is the damage done by an economic system geared towards short-term profit maximization – from those who bear the responsibility for the system to the general public. Seen in this context, human "happiness" could become a guiding principle for future European policy.

When looking at the quality of life of people in Europe, it is important to consider the area of work. Whether people have a job or not is one of the core factors determining whether they feel happy or not. In addition to ecological aspects of sustainability, in this case we are primarily concerned with the social side of sustainability.

Paid labor and happiness

Together with income and consumption (of goods and services), work (paid and unpaid) and other (recreational) activities that focus on intellectual and emotional experiences (for

Measuring happiness

Can human happiness be measured – and if so, how? For some years, noted scientific institutions have concerned themselves with measuring human happiness in different countries. Subjective satisfaction with life, for example, is determined by directly surveying the population, for example in the *General Social Survey* in the USA, or in the so-called *Eurobarometer*. In Germany, the renowned *Allensbach Institute* has been studying the well-being of the population for years; in Great Britain, the *New Economics Foundation* concerns itself with this question.

Neuroscience provides us with further clues. When test subjects are shown positive stimuli (for example funny film excerpts or beautiful pictures), certain areas of the left front part of the brain (cortex) become measurably active. When shown negative stimuli (for example horrible photos), the right side is activated instead. Scientists have been able to prove that people with a particularly active left cortex are more satisfied with life (see Layard). There is further evidence for a connection between objectively observable features and subjective self-assessment. People who describe themselves as very satisfied smile more and are less likely to commit suicide. The interviewees' self-assessment also correlates with the assessment by friends and relatives.

The economists Kahneman and Krueger (2006) chose another method of measuring happiness; they asked how much time each subject of the study spent in a subjectively unpleasant state. To measure this, over a certain period of time, subjects had to keep a diary of all their activities and rate the feelings associated with each action. Some of the feelings listed are positive (happy, self-satisfied, friendly), others are negative (depressed, angry, frustrated). When a negative feeling is assigned the highest value in a particular situation, the researchers consider this period unpleasant.

The Dutch happiness researcher Veenhoven, on the other hand, suggests compiled indicators to compare the happiness of nations: *Happy Life Expectancy*. He uses the World Value Survey, in which citizens rate their happiness on a scale of one to ten. The average is converted into values between zero and one and then multiplied by the average life expectancy. Veenhoven interprets the result as follows: the longer and the happier people live, the better the rights and duties anchored in a society fit the needs and abilities of its citizens. Currently, Switzerland has the highest 'happy life expectancy' at sixty-three years. Moldova has the lowest at 20.5 years.

In addition to approaches that measure subjective well-being, there are many further approaches that attempt the objective measurement of prosperity and then subtract the amount of the gross national product spent on social ills (criminality, environmental cleanup, expenditures for sick people). Attempts have also been made to quantify activities that are not included in the gross domestic product, such as free time or work in the family. Examples of this are the *Genuine Progress Indicator* or the *Measure of Domestic Progress,* as proposed by the New Economics Foundation in London. On measuring happiness, see for example well-known economists Richard Layard and Bruno Frey. Jordis Grimm provides an overall view on the subject in German.

example being together with others, cultural activities, experiencing nature, and meditating) contribute to the satisfaction of human needs.

To be "unemployed" (the term "without gainful employment" would be better) is a very negative experience for most who go through it. Concurrent to losing their place of paid employment, people often have the feeling of no longer being needed in society – up to and including the loss of concrete social contacts and relationships. Jobs fulfill not only an economic, but also a social function: participation in social life.

Work therefore not only generates an income with which we can satisfy our material desires, but also contributes directly to our well-being. On the other hand, other activities also add to our happiness and the happiness of others. These include spending time with our children, partners, and friends; caring for the old and sick; being active in our neighborhood or in social or political organizations, as well as the enjoyment of culture and many other non-work related contributions to self-fulfillment. Increasingly, these are doomed to failure due to the "stress" caused by our gainful employment. Today it seems – thanks to an enormous increase in productivity – that the "core" of society in part already has too many private and public goods, and at the same time lacks the time and energy to make suitable use of them; perhaps one could call this "relationship poverty" with concomitant private and public prosperity. Put a bit more technically: there is a lack of social capital (see Putnam). This lack of social capital is the bane particularly of those who have full-time gainful employment, whereby those people with no gainful employment feel their situation to be negative, but on the whole could have more social capital at their disposal.

Satisfying and fulfilling gainful employment for everyone who wants it is an important component of social sustainability.

What is human and social capital?

In Chapter 3, we saw that we can think of nature as a form of capital – similar to machines, infrastructures, and financial means – necessary to the production of our prosperity. Without pushing this analogy too far, it does show us that we must not live from the principal itself, but rather from the "interest" in order to live a good life long-term.

Alongside "natural capital," there are however further forms of wealth needed for an economy to be competitive: human capital and social capital. The OECD realized this some years ago and has instituted projects in its member states to measure these forms of capital. The most well-known are probably the so-called PISA studies on the quality of scholastic performance. Our educational system produces, so to speak, "human capital," or the quality of human labor. Of course, education is much more than just the capital necessary to the economy. However, without highly qualified laborers, in the long term an economy will not be able to hold its own against other parts of the world.

Newer and less well-known is the OECD work on "social capital." In Austria, Ernst Gehmacher, the grand old man of Austrian social research, is working on this problem. Social capital, according to the work published by Gehmacher in collaboration with Kroismayr and Neumüller, always has two facets: "bonding" within a "social entity," such as a family, company, country, or the world; and the relationship to other social entities, either above or outside the first: "bridging." This social capital is currently decreasing virtually everywhere in the world. We're living on the interest of earlier cultural developments, which in the end will have to have an effect on the economic development of those countries that do not manage to develop effective strategies to rebuild their social capital.

However, industrialized societies obviously have their problems with fulfilling this need.

The second half of the 20th century was at first character-ized by a large number of "normal jobs" (forty hours per week, forty weeks per year, forty years of one's life), particularly for the male segment of society. This state of affairs was supported and cemented by the reigning (Social Democratic or Conservative) social and economic policy as well as by collective wage agree-ments; while women at first worked primarily in the family and home and dominated only in specific areas of working life (for example, the textile industry, retailing, and education).

On the other hand, there are clear shortfalls in the supply of social services on the ever larger margins of society. For about thirty years, the social welfare system has been crumbling due on the one hand to a larger number of unemployed people (while at the same time more women and migrants have joined the labor force), and on the other hand (and connected to the former) to the increase in so-called "atypical jobs" (part-time with no benefits, freelance contracts, etc.) and irregular job his-tories. The latter means that increasingly, people have phases of (voluntary or involuntary) unemployment as well as phases of gainful employment, which also leads to a less equal distribution of income and wealth over time. For the core of society, which is becoming smaller and smaller, participation in the labor market is increasing (these people are working and earning more), while more and more holes are eaten into the "social net," which is based on the model of "normal work."

At the same time, the "social welfare system" (understood here very broadly, including financing the educational system, cultural institutions, etc.) is becoming more and more expensive; on the one hand because fewer and fewer people can participate in financing it at any given time, and on the other hand because the demands upon the system are becoming greater rather than smaller.

A holistic view of labor: mixed work

To do justice to current labor market developments, it helps to expand our thinking about what "labor" means, away from "normal" paid employment towards a holistic view, that of so-called "mixed work." The concept of mixed work, developed at the Social Science Research Center in Berlin, places paid labor in a broader context including all forms of unpaid work relevant to the economy; such as work for oneself (for example house-work and gardening), care (for example childcare and caring for the sick and aged), and community work (for example volunteer work in self-help groups, informal organizations, and charities) and recognizes all of this informal labor as a productive con-tribution to the sustainability of our society. Our current eco-nomic system continues to take unpaid activities, which lay an important foundation for our economy, for granted as the unval-ued preconditions of our existence. In the mixed work concept, this important labor is explicitly taken into account and thus more value is placed on it (see Brandl and Hildebrandt as well as Stocker, Hinterberger and Strasser).

Gainful employment remains the dominant concept, but it is reduced over the course of an entire average life – as well as over the average work week. The well-known German statistician Carsten Stahmer coined the provocative term "part-time society" in this context (see Schaffer and Stahner). If we look at the rela-tionship between paid and unpaid labor, we see that 56 billion hours of paid work and 96 billion hours of unpaid labor were performed in Germany in 2001. The 96 billion unpaid hours of labor are divided unequally between men and women. According to the German Federal Statistical Office, men performed 22.5 hours of paid labor on average per week in 2003, and women only twelve hours. Conversely, men did 19.5 hours of unpaid work, while women worked thirty hours without pay each week.

Seen this way, normal employment is anything but "normal," rather it is the exception. On the other hand, the "normality" of normal employment often calls for many hours of overtime, leaving little free time for unpaid work. This development forces us to think about a different form of distributing labor. Not only are the usual working hours and the compensation of overtime up for discussion, but also longer vacation time and the expansion of leaves and sabbaticals. Lowering the retirement age (shortening the total number of hours worked in a person's life) is less desirable from a sustainability perspective, for a variety of reasons (financing retirement plans, making mixed work possible, participation in social life).

On the contrary: the part-time society is a form of mixed work in which the amount of paid labor for every individual is reduced on a voluntary basis and time and space is given for community involvement. Older and younger people, who have a lot of personal free time, can utilize their potential for involvement in the community apart from paid labor. Less individual time spent at paid employment for each individual gives others who are able and willing to work the chance to participate in the labor market.

In this way, not only can less paid work be divided among more people, but also more time for learning, relationships, self-fulfillment, care of children and dependents, or community involvement becomes available for those who are currently working to exhaustion. This allows not only a voluntary reduction of material consumption in favor of more free time, but also more (life)time to actively commit to the goals of sustainable development.

Companies such as the Austrian furniture maker and mail order company "Grüne Erde," as well as BMW, the drugstore chain DM, or Zeiss in Jena are demonstrating that flexible working hours in no way contradict a company's profit interests, while others are still opposed to the very idea. Utilizing available labor efficiently is a question of how a company is organized internally. Just as eco-efficiency pays, so does companies' responding flexibly to the needs of their employees.

Furthermore, it is also a question of responsibility for every single company or manager whether they allow people to participate in the labor market or let millions of people go, leaving them unemployed. Currently, however, many social and labor law regulations work against utilizing this potential in a comprehensive manner. They're still written for the "normal employment relationship" of the 20th century.

We have seen that it is not only nature that has no price, but also most of the work done in our society, making it, in the eyes of many, of little or no 'value.' In the 21st century, paid labor is still distributed very unequally between men and women, between people of different ages, and between different social strata. The fact that labor and income are distributed unevenly also means that those people who do have an income from gainful employment need to spend an ever greater portion of it to pay for the professional execution of many social tasks (from care to environmental protection) – either directly or in the form of taxes and charges levied by the state in order to finance the provision of these services. These fees in turn raise the cost of labor. The result is that it becomes more and more expensive to hire people, and more jobs are eliminated by technical rationalization.

This vicious circle could be broken, for more and more people want to work less in their lifetimes in order to have more time for other things. They would be all too happy to make room for others who have no jobs – and they would also "use" less of the environment, because since they earned less, they would consume less. Redistributing the work that needs to be done, work in offices and factories as well as in nurseries and homes, could also help; alongside more part-time jobs, more flexibility on the job, more sabbaticals, and more paternity leave. The positive results would be: increased productivity at work, more personal touches in (personal) care, which in turn could be better interlocked with help from teachers and professional caretakers. In a nutshell: social sustainability includes transforming the social value of labor from exclusively gainful employment to mixed work.

In this context, full employment doesn't mean a return to "normal employment for all," but rather a situation in which all those who want to perform paid labor are able to find a job. This requires a certain amount of flexibility on all sides, but would also have the advantage of giving many people currently categorized as poorly qualified the opportunity to become qualified on the job – or to have an incentive to become qualified in the first place.

If we decouple social progress from economic growth, restructuring labor in this way could contribute to qualitative progress and further development towards sustainability. Rather than more economic prosperity, this form of progress would create more "happiness." Less economic growth or even "zero growth" could admittedly be the result of less gainful employment. However, less economic growth, measured by gross domestic product, also means less interference in natural systems.

How realistic is the vision of a sustainable society?

A better life and jobs for many do not necessarily have to come at nature's expense and thus at the expense of generations to come and of people in the Third World. Just because we'd like to see such a world, however, doesn't mean it's also possible. In fact, the view of social progress presented above is often denounced as "wishful thinking" that doesn't pay off economically.

Particularly in recent years, however, model calculations have shown that positive developments in the sense of the social goals postulated above are possible on a macroeconomic scale; although there are sure to be "losers" in the transition period, particularly among those who, due to their economic and personal conditions, are less able to adapt to the new requirements.

We would like to call the reader's attention to two research projects in which we have been involved: A joint project commissioned by the Hans Böckler Foundation examined these questions in detail for Germany. The project was executed by the Wuppertal Institute in cooperation with the German Institute for Economic Research (see http://www.a-und-oe.de/verbund/start-frm.htm for a sixty-page English summary). At the European level, the MOSUS project (www.mosus.net) reached conclusions very similar to the ideas presented here. This project, funded by the European Commission, simulated scenarios for Europe's development towards sustainability between the present and the year 2020. The main conclusion of the project was that a combination of different environmental policy instruments geared towards increasing energy and material efficiency would have positive effects both on economic development and on the environment.

The most important conclusion was that environmental policy measures that aim to decouple material and energy consumption from economic growth can also be catalysts for economic growth – in contrast to popular opinion that believes these policy measures raise production costs for companies and thus lower competitiveness. This gives us room to do even more for environmental protection, particularly because, as we have shown, economic growth contributes only little to social well-being.

5 Paths towards Sustainability

Let us sum up what we have elaborated so far: Global change is taking place to an extent that threatens the foundation of life on Earth. Global change must not be equated with climate change, it is much more than that alone. Human activities transform the Earth' surface, biological diversity, the quantity and quality of drinking water, the oceans, and much more. To complicate things further, Earth is a complex and interconnected system. We need to understand this system in order to ensure that our interventions lead to the results we desire. Since, however, we have already caused undesirable changes, we must adapt to them and take measures that reduce further negative impacts. In general, we have to limit our interference with natural systems to a level that guarantees the ecologically responsible use of nature rather than exhausting natural capital. For this to occur, a dramatic improvement in resource efficiency is necessary. To achieve sustainable development for our planet, we therefore need an efficiency strategy that results in this improvement. Moreover, we can also promote the goal of sustainable development by changes in our lifestyle. When we no longer automatically see social progress as coupled to economic growth, but rather as a true improvement in the quality of our lives, we are supporting sustainable development.

This chapter deals with ways in which we can reach the goals outlined above. It is only an excerpt of the current discourse and does not aspire to completeness. Importantly, there is no *single* path towards sustainability. Only a combination of many measures and activities by policy-makers, business, and each individual person will begin to lead us forward on the path towards sustainability.

Admittedly, the difficulties begin when it comes to concrete measures. Sustainability as a guiding principle is incorporated within many existing national and international documents, but as soon as the focus is on fixing the details of implementation or on making this guiding principle concrete, differences emerge. Diverse stakeholders' goals and strategies as well as the scope of their activities often diverge sharply. Even if many countries have committed almost unanimously to the main goal of "sustainable development," concretization and implementation are still far away. Nevertheless, we would like to delineate the most important opportunities for action below.

From environmental policy to resource policy

Dramatic improvement of resource efficiency cannot be achieved by relying on individual people and companies to rethink and change their actions. It is necessary to provide proper political and economic incentives to ensure that individuals and companies get the right signals and invest in resource-saving technologies or innovative services.

The main goal of environmental and economic policy must be to ensure that the prices of natural resources and products send the right signals.

The new environmental policy: prevention, not cure

In the past three decades, environmental awareness has improved greatly in Europe. This growing understanding of the dangers of increased human interference with the environment has intensified pressure on political actors. However, whether or not environmental policy measures can prevail over other policy concerns still depends upon the perception of concrete problems at the regional level. The visibility and perceptible urgency of certain environmental problems makes it easier to push through political measures (to fight air and water pollution, for example). Technologies known today as "end-of-pipe" measures were employed to reduce these environmental impacts. Examples of such measures include filters on smokestacks or catalytic converters in cars. At the same time, long-term environmental problems are pushed into the background by such short-term measures as long as their impacts are not perceived as dramatic enough (for example climate change, loss of biodiversity). In the light of this tension between short-term emergency activities and long-term strategic goals, environmental policy has long limited itself primarily to after-the-fact measures, namely cleanup of acute environmental burdens. Precautionary measures have been, on the other hand, neglected.

Meanwhile, the view that environmental policy should concentrate on the underlying causes of the problem and not simply on dealing with the consequences is beginning to gain the upper hand. The basic idea is quite simple: less input (consumption of nature) leads to less output (environmental impact).

Even if there is still no comprehensive resource policy for Europe, there have been many promising efforts. For example, Austria, the Netherlands, Sweden, Finland, and Japan have integrated this environmental policy concept into their sustainability programs. Germany has also defined concrete goals for resource efficiency in its sustainability strategy. On the European level, these developments are taken into account in the 6th Environment Action Programme, which is currently in effect. Although the implementation of these programs still needs improvement in many areas, we can see that a new principle of environmental policy has taken root: Prevention, not cure.

Which specific political instruments can be implemented to reduce resource consumption? In principle, it is possible to categorize policy measures in this area according to how strongly they interfere with companies' and consumers' individual decisions. We can distinguish three types: regulatory requirements and bans, economic incentives, and voluntary measures. Many things speak for a combination of all three instruments – for in the interaction of environment and society we are confronted with numerous complex problems that call for a variety of problem-solving approaches.

Command and control

Regulatory requirements and bans are among the classic environmental policy instruments. Clear rules of behavior are imposed upon a company (or a consumer), whereby non-compliance is always linked to the threat of sanctions. Also known as "command and control measures," their main function is to guarantee a certain minimum standard, for example emission ceilings for certain pollutants. Concerning the reduction of resource consumption, rules on the quality or quantity of material input, on processing norms, or the specification of permissible technologies are also important.

The new economic policy

The task for political decision-makers must be to design the framework conditions for competition in a manner that makes it attractive for companies to develop resource-saving products and process innovations. It is illusory to believe that the government can force the development of such innovations through direct intervention. One need only recall the complete failure of centrally-planned socialist economies to accomplish technical progress. The government can only make the rules and provide incentives; it should not, however, become an active player and certainly should not dominate the game.

Examples of incentives are taxes on resource consumption and tradable resource use allowances (environmental permits) allocated to companies by the government that businesses can then trade amongst themselves (see below). These incentives are meant to encourage companies to make use of existing opportunities to reduce resource use and, in particular, to develop innovative resource-saving technologies. For the consumer, the result is that all consumer goods that directly or indirectly cause high resource consumption become more expensive. Therefore a car produced in a manner that uses more fossil fuels, more ore, and more non-mineral raw materials will be more expensive than another, lighter, car made from steel produced from scrap "burnt" in an electric arc furnace, whereby the electricity in turn is gained from renewable sources. A market that taxes resource consumption steers the economic necessity of lowering costs in the right direction. At the same time, producers are provided with incentives to make consumer goods that use up less of the environment.

In addition to taxes, fees or levies on environmental consumption that would have to be integrated into the costing of products and services are also conceivable. However, it remains an individual decision left to people or companies to search out the adaptation measure best suited to their needs. This promotes creative solutions, because innovations that create more resource efficiency pay off in the end.

One important approach among the market-oriented mechanisms is ecological tax reform. It aims at shifting the tax burden so that environmental consumption is taxed and other areas, such as labor, can be relieved of their tax burdens. There are two main approaches to ecotaxation:

– *Energy taxes*, rudimentary forms of which can already be found in many European Union countries, are relatively easy to implement due to the small number of energy carriers.
– *Material input taxes*, or taxing all resource flows are, in contrast, somewhat more difficult to administer. However, here too, some promising first steps have already been taken.

Both models can help send the right price signals to consumers. After all, higher prices for energy and material input work their way along the production chain to the consumer, so that the more economical alternative will have a much better price. Experience shows that incremental increases of these taxes are advisable, in order to give business and consumers enough time to adapt.

If we are aiming for widespread and harmonized sustainability policy, we must also subject the current subsidy system to a critical examination. On the one hand, subsidies can promote environmentally-friendly technologies; on the other hand, they can also, in the form of so-called "perverse subsidies," harm both the economy and the environment in the long term. Some examples are the subsidies for diesel and coal, and the tax exemption for

How emissions trading works

The goal of emissions trading is the economically most efficient distribution of a set (by governments) amount of dangerous emissions with long-range or global effects. Therefore, the emissions permits distributed by the government give companies the right to a certain amount of emissions (for example one metric ton of carbon dioxide). The total number of permits distributed within a certain time period is fixed (capped) and is determined by the emissions reduction target. Businesses may trade permits as they wish, whereby the price is determined by supply and demand on the free market. Companies that need more certificates must buy them from other companies that need fewer because they have already largely fulfilled their reduction commitments. The companies may thus decide for themselves how quickly or slowly they want to fulfill their reduction commitments and can adapt their innovation plans to include the necessary technical conversions.

kerosene. These subsidies not only encourage resource consumption, they also delay conversion to renewable energy sources. The same can be said of financial aid for intensive agriculture (as well as for the use of pesticides), grant schemes for home buyers, and tax write-offs for commuters. The reasons given for the implementation of these measures are diverse; usually, though, no environmental impact assessment is carried out. If, however, we desire to reach our environmental policy goals, a careful analysis of the effects of subsidies is indispensible. We must aim to support activities that improve efficiency for a limited period of time and to abolish subsidies for non-sustainable activities as far as possible. Altogether, we are talking about considerable monetary sums, which also affect taxes and budget deficits.

Another interesting approach is installing a system of *tradable permits*. Similar to the regulation of carbon dioxide emissions by the Kyoto Protocol, so-called "material input permits" – tradable property rights for natural resources – could be created with set ceilings of an agreed-upon amount. In this case as well, the total amounts could be reduced incrementally in order to give companies enough time to adapt.

Education and support

Political measures can, even must, be supported by educational programs that contribute to bringing about changes in people's behavior. Campaigns for the dissemination of information, education, and the support of public dialogue on long-term perspectives can help strengthen society's willingness to act, as well as build competency in environmental and societal questions. These programs also should include support for research and development on environmentally sound technical and social progress.

Voluntary agreements

On the European level, in addition to the measures described above, voluntary environmental agreements entered into by businesses to reduce their resource consumption are playing an increasingly important role. This can pay off in more ways than one: not only does reducing material consumption save on costs, but it can also obviate the necessity for legal regulations, whose implementation is often linked to high costs for companies.

Nevertheless, the effectiveness of voluntary measures is very controversial. How much do voluntary business commitments differ from normal production processes in the end? And how much can you influence the behavior of individuals by educational campaigns?

The right mix

Only a wise combination of the different instruments described above can lead towards sustainability. Depending on the situation, different approaches can be combined in order to develop appropriate problem-solving strategies. Regulatory requirements and bans are useful in particular to react quickly to problems concerning the use of certain resources. On the other hand, due to their lack of flexibility, their implementation is sometimes not ideally suited to the circumstances of individual companies. In contrast, economic incentives and voluntary measures allow for more flexibility in the design of individual environmentally sound adaptation. Particularly in order to lower total energy and material consumption in the long term, these measures are indispensible as supplements to legal regulations. In any case, all measures taken should be the result of a transparent political process which, within the framework of a societal consensus, takes economic, social, and environmental goals into account.

Fair play in the global economy

Although the global economy is growing continuously and humankind as a whole is becoming more affluent, the profits of globalization are, to an ever greater proportion, concentrated in the hands of the rich segments of the population. Especially many developing countries fail to benefit from the increasing interconnection of the global economy and from the fast growth of international trade. In many of these countries, the per capita income is even lower today than it was in 1980.

This development is neither economically, nor socially, nor environmentally sustainable. But what do we have to change so that the profits of globalization are distributed more fairly between the different regions of the world?

From the point of view of a developing country, the most important long-term goal towards establishing sustainable economic structures is to reduce the dependency of economic development on the export of (usually unprocessed) raw materials. This is important because on the one hand, raw materials are subject to enormous price swings on the global commodities markets and, on the other hand, they generate less income than the sale of more processed products (for example machine or computer parts). One important economic development goal is therefore not to export domestically produced products as raw materials, but to process them, increase their value, and thus also obtain higher prices.

However, the massive interests of industrialized countries stand in the way of this goal – despite all the rhetoric about liberalized world trade. Whereas the industrialized countries are pushing the developing countries to quickly open their markets to industrial products, many of their own important economic sectors, such as agriculture, but also industry, remain protected

Political measures to increase resource efficiency

Both the environment and the economy can benefit from
the right mix of instruments. An overview of the most
important instruments:

- Shifting the tax burden in the course of an ecological
  tax reform away from labor and towards resource
  consumption.
- Eliminating subsidies that encourage the overuse of
  natural resources in the sectors of agriculture, fishing,
  transportation, and energy.
- Supporting research and technology development
  to increase the resource efficiency of products and
  production methods.
- Introducing targets to improve resource efficiency in
  public procurement as well as company environmental
  reporting.
- Binding minimum standards for the average energy
  use of products (consumption ceilings for household
  appliances or cars).
- Value-added tax exemptions for products with
  recognized labels such as environmental labels, organic
  products, and fair trade products.
- New spatial planning measures that bring all spheres
  of life back together: housing, working, and shopping.

from increasing competition from the South by tariffs and other barriers. Reports by the non-governmental organization Oxfam from 2002 show that import tariffs in the industrialized countries for goods from developing countries are on average around four times as high as those for exports from the North to the South.

Rich industrialized countries never tire of saying that free trade is the best instrument in the fight against poverty in the developing countries. However, this can only function if a fair and balanced international trade system is established which not only does not discriminate against the poorest countries but also actively supports them by means of special regulations (for example tariff-free access to the markets of industrialized countries). More justice in the global economy can only be achieved if strong nations carry the greater burden in the world trade system and weak nations receive preferential treatment. Support for fair trade products is an important step in this direction, because they enable the people who make products such as coffee or cocoa to receive a fair price and thus also help reduce poverty in the producer countries.

A further important point is the fact that in developing countries, economic sectors such as mining and agriculture are usually controlled by multinational enterprises. For example, just three companies (Chiquita, Dole, and Del Monte) control more than 70% of global banana production. These companies act in the interest of the industrialized countries, and they can transfer the profits made from the extraction and sale of raw materials to the companies' home countries. Therefore, one important measure would be to establish international regulations that oblige multinational enterprises to reinvest a larger proportion of their profits in the country of production. Tax revenues could then be used to support important areas such as health and education systems, which are the foundation of successful economic development and the fight against poverty.

One important initiative for a new cooperation to create security, peace, and prosperity for all people on Earth is the so-called "Global Marshall Plan." The aim of the Global Marshall Plan, initiated in 2003, is a "world in balance." This demands actively designing the workings of globalization and global economic processes. The overriding goal of the initiative is the so-called "eco-social market economy," an economic framework which takes non-economic goals into account and supports them: poverty alleviation, environmental protection, and global justice. One central approach of the Global Marshall Plan is financial support from the rich countries for projects in developing countries under the condition that ecological and social standards are met, as for example was done in the eastern enlargement of the European Union. In this way, environmental and social dumping can be prevented, something which would benefit both the rich and the poor countries in the medium and long term.

The Global Marshall Plan Initiative works towards three main goals:

- Rapid implementation of the globally agreed-upon United Nations Millennium Development Goals (see Chapter 1) as an interim step to a just world order and sustainable development.
- Raising an additional 100 billion US dollars annually for development aid between 2008 and 2015. In addition to national funding sources, this money should be raised in a fair manner that does not distort competition, for example taxes on global financial transactions (the so-called Tobin Tax), or on goods traded on the global market.
- Incremental realization of a worldwide eco-social market economy by establishing a global economic framework (a fair 'global agreement'). This agreement is to link and

expand upon existing policies and agreed-upon institutional standards (particularly within the United Nations system). The main goal of this framework is to require polluters to pay for the costs of environmental impacts (true environmental costs). Only in this manner can the power of the markets be harnessed and steered towards sustainability.

The power of sufficiency

Sustainability cannot be achieved with improved efficiency and (technical) innovations alone (see Chapter 4), certainly not if we take into account the population growth the UN predicts for the coming years as well as the increase in consumer demands. If we are to succeed at living together in a crowded world in an environmentally-friendly and social manner, then we must curb our demands – in other words: sufficiency is necessary.

Prosperous societies need to limit themselves, for without limitations we will be unable to preserve the natural foundation of our existence in the long-term. What is more, if we fail to preserve the natural foundations of our existence, we will in principle not be able to attain a peaceful balance between poor and rich. However, sufficiency is not exactly an idea taken up excitedly in social discourse – to the contrary.

Usually, and incorrectly, it is linked to scarcity and asceticism. Yet sufficiency can lead to a new understanding of prosperity and progress and help us to better determine the relationship between material goods and immaterial needs. "Sufficiency" means being content with that which is adequate. "Adequate", in turn, can be defined as everything which is not too much. If we take human well-being (or happiness) as the decisive measure of adequacy (for beyond a certain level of material prosperity there is no significant increase in well-being, see Chapter 4), then the industrialized countries have considerable potential for increasing sufficiency and improving the quality of life simultaneously.

An increase in sufficiency can be supported by governments setting the necessary frameworks, but also by companies that turn away from mass production and devote themselves to the actual needs of their customers.

Governments face the challenge of rejecting the superficial demand for a permanently growing economy and seeking alternatives together with their citizens, alternatives which can achieve "full employment" and a high quality of life for all of society.

The individual or consumer level is also of utmost importance if we are to avoid "too much." Surplus becomes dangerous at the moment when the (over)fulfillment of one need prevents the fulfillment of other needs, even those necessary for our long-term survival, and when ethical principles are disregarded. Seen this way, sufficiency can contribute to a temperate and happier life: instead of material surplus, fulfillment of immaterial needs and more justice between rich and poor.

Measures towards sustainable development must also include a new organization of employment (see Chapter 4). The concept of mixed work shows that our working lives are made up of more than just paid labor (which is of course very important), the amount of which is shrinking. Other forms of work, such as volunteer and community work in groups and non-profit organizations, caring for relatives and friends, as well as indispensible "time for oneself," for education and personal development, are as plentiful as ever. What we should aspire to is known as a "work-life balance." Realizing this balance is both a political and societal task and a challenge for each and every individual.

A redistribution of labor between paid and unpaid work has to be accompanied by a mechanism to secure income. The good

Negative income tax: how it works

A negative income tax means that, according to their income, citizens either pay positive taxes or are paid a negative tax (receive transfer payments). There is a successive decrease of transfer payments as a person's income increases; when a certain limit is reached, the person must then begin to pay taxes. In this system, the "guaranteed basic income" that today exists in the form of social welfare is combined with the taxation system. This allows a simplification of the social security system, particularly in the areas of income maintenance, emergency aid, and unemployment benefits.

Currently there is a tax rate (more exactly: transfer reduction rate) of 100% when a recipient of unemployment or social welfare benefits takes a part-time job. This means that people often earn less working than they received in benefits; not a real incentive to work. With a negative income tax, a portion of the transfer could be kept, up to a certain limit; the earned income would be taxed only partially. This is not only a less bureaucratic social welfare system, but also provides more incentive for people receiving social benefits to take on work. Furthermore, the system would support mixed work, because the border between paid and unpaid labor would be more permeable (compare for example Hüther, 1990).

One common objection to the broadening, intensification, and monetary increase of basic income is that income is in and of itself an incentive to take on a job. The fact that the majority of work (for example housework, child care, and sickbed care) is currently completely unpaid and nevertheless gets done contradicts this hypothesis.

Nevertheless, we can see that many satisfying and meaningful working opportunities are not taken up, because people cannot afford to do so. This is similarly true for start-up businesses, as they are under a lot of pressure to make a profit as quickly as possible.

What is true, however, is that a basic income would put pressure on wages in low-income sectors. This is not only true for jobs that do not require many skills (for example work as a supermarket cashier), but also for the care and education of young children, and jobs in the health care sector.

life requires financial security in the form of a basic income for all so that unpaid work is affordable. A basic income in the form of a negative income tax would provide the financing needed to initiate and realize new approaches to work in the currently understaffed and underfinanced community sector – even if only on a comparatively low level.

Policy-level implementation

Why is it so difficult to provide a catalyst for sustainable development? What do we need to do, which tools can we employ? There are at least two different levels on which implementation has to take place. We make a distinction between the collective and the individual level. Let us begin with the collective, or policy, level.

Our social system is constantly in flux. It is increasingly difficult for decision-makers in politics, administration, business, and civil society organizations to find an audience for their concerns and interests in an increasingly complex world. Former steering mechanisms such as, for example, hierarchical spatial planning or governmental regulatory requirements and bans are less and less able to meet current demands and are losing more and more of their significance.

The term *governance* was coined as a way to depict the collective, policy-making, level. In the broadest sense, it means the mechanisms and rules by which socio-political systems are managed.

The conditions for managing societal development are changing at an ever-increasing speed. The world economy is turning towards a global orientation, leading to an increase in the influence of global enterprises and economic steering mechanisms. Non-government organizations, too, are increasingly working in global networks. Local actors find themselves embedded in a worldwide context; many act not only on the local, but also on the global level. Furthermore, many problems do not stop at national borders. There is an increasing gap between the level at which problems occur and the policy level; nation-states are faced with the challenge of finding solutions for problems which do not end at their borders, such as, for example, environmental problems. What then are the concrete levels at which all stakeholders act, summarized by the term governance?

Global governance – world order policy

Concepts for a new world order policy are being discussed under the term *global governance*. More and more often the question arises whether global governing bodies need to be strengthened in times of globalization. Networking on a variety of levels, flexible steering mechanisms, and subsidiarity are the central criteria for the design of the emerging global governance concept. The nation-state is not to be replaced, but rather transformed into a coordinating state.

The goal is the political design of global change – with the aim of ensuring that all people and our environment can make the most out of the opportunities globalization offers, minimizing its risks and correcting its current undesirable developments. An interesting study published by the Forum Sustainable Austria (2006) assumes that this can only be successful if we are able to overcome the current power imbalances that prevent us from building global partnerships to solve global problems. If the purpose of the economy is to serve the global community and make full development, conservation, and preservation of life possible; then we need frameworks which support this, such as those propagated by the regulatory concept of the eco-social market economy and the Global Marshall Plan (see above).

Global governance not only means setting new frameworks and more intense cooperation in international organizations; it is also a broadly conceived, dynamic process of consensus-finding and decision-making.

The national level and the EU level

The main concern in all discussions about governance in the public sector is the search for a new role for nation-states, regions, and the European Union. One contribution to this discussion, still important today, is the EU Commission's paper *European Governance. A White Paper* (2001). In it, the Commission makes its wishes known for a reform of European governance and also delineates the contributions Member States can make. The paper introduced five guiding principles for the reform: openness, participation, accountability, effectiveness, and coherence. The three key proposals for change are:

– Involving the populace more in decision-making on all levels
– Greater flexibility of policy instruments
– Overall policy coherence.

The EU's main goal is to implement new steering mechanisms in order to solve problems such as a general lack of interest in politics or the fact that EU political and administrative bodies are seen as institutions detached from the realities of daily life. Because of this, the general public has voted in referenda not to accept the proposed European Constitution and, more recently, the Irish referendum turned down the Lisbon Treaty. The search for the role of nation-states, regions and the European Union continues, and the debate on ways to achieve the overriding goals of involving the general public in decision-making processes and making the expanded European Union effective goes on.

Happy Europe?

"Happiness of the people" could be the new overriding goal for a "new" Europe – similar to the statement made in "old" America's Declaration of Independence. This declaration, on which the American constitution is based, states "that all men are created equal, that they are endowed by their creator with certain unalienable rights, that among these are Life, Liberty and the pursuit of Happiness."

Ever since the draft of a European Union constitution was voted down in referendums in France and the Netherlands, the proposal has often been made that a constitution acceptable to the majority of Europeans would have to be much shorter and deal with people's central concerns. The Lisbon Treaty is indeed shorter but has still not achieved universal acceptance. What seems to be needed is a framework within which people in Europe – as well as in other parts of the world – would be best able to pursue happiness.

Rather than looking together towards the future and tackling the profound problems facing us, statesmen (and those few stateswomen) of all political persuasions spend their time on mutual accusations about whose policies are to blame for our misery, particularly for high unemployment. Thus farmers are played off against workers, the unemployed against business, and economic policy against environmental and social policy.

Seen this way, it would be the task of political, administrative, and economic decision-makers to act in their respective sectors to support people, helping them to find satisfaction in life and realize their full potential. In addition to supporting individual skills, this also means creating and maintaining the natural and social systems necessary to our survival. All people should be as happy as possible and the distribution of happiness should be as just as possible – within each generation and over a longer period of time for many generations to come. In this model, work and income are only means to an end. This is in accordance with the fundamental principle of sustainability: reconciling ecology, economy, and social services on a high level.

A first step in this direction was made with the agreement on the European Sustainability Development Strategy at the Gothenburg Summit in 2001. Fundamentally revised and ratified by the twenty-five EU state and government leaders in June 2006, it states: "The overall aim of the renewed EU Sustainable Development Strategy is to identify and develop actions to enable the EU to achieve continuous improvement of quality of life both for current and for future generations, through the creation of sustainable communities able to manage and use resources efficiently and to tap the ecological and social innovation potential of the economy, ensuring prosperity, environmental protection and social cohesion."

The local level

On the local level of governance in particular, there have been many diverse explorations of new approaches in the past years. Many efforts have been and still are being made to adapt policy and steering mechanisms such as spatial planning, to transform them from very hierarchical to participative instruments (in which the population takes part in decision-making processes), sometimes even using environmental mediation, in order to meet changing demands. The spread of globalization also plays a role in this. Decisions made on the local or regional level have an effect upon other decision-making levels far away and vice versa. People also often act not only on the local level, but also on the (trans)regional and global level. Unlike global governance and governance on the national or EU level, usually discussed in an environmental or economic policy context, the spatial dimension is also important in local governance. Governance geared towards sustainable development can be operationalized and implemented on the regional level in particular. Within this process, the definition of "region" changes depending on the current needs to be met or problems to be solved. There have been a variety of approaches at this level of governance in recent years (for example Local Agenda 21 processes) that have been increasingly recognized by policy-makers and administrations and have led to the formation of new structures of governance.

Strengthening civil society

There is general agreement that sustainable development requires an increased appreciation of civil society involvement. This trend began with the new networks and movements which formed on the periphery of traditional political movements. A strong civil society serves a better balance between a strong economy and weakening nation-states.

Non-governmental organizations play an important role in strengthening civil society. Their most important characteristic and their greatest asset, whether we are looking at Greenpeace or a local citizens' group, is their independence from political institutions and business lobbyists. Despite the great significance that an active civil society and citizens' contributions to society have already gained, there are still many opportunities for development. Better information, improved communication between groups, and mobilizing more people could lead to an even stronger civil society.

Transition management

Sustainable development means change, dynamics, and social transformation. In other words: transition. Therefore, implementing "sustainability" as a guiding principle also means making fundamental changes in our current consumption, production, and decision-making habits.

Social transition is based on the dynamics of interlinked changes, for example in the socio-political levels described above – not only in relation to patterns of political action and decision-making. Such dynamics are also based on interconnected changes in the areas of technology, economy, institutions, behavior, culture, value systems, or environmental frameworks. In this context, when policy-makers want to intervene and steer the course of society, they face the challenge of the interdependencies of socio-economic systems and the concurrent factors of uncertainties that affect their decision-making processes. Due to the complexity and mutual dependencies of the different systems, it is impossible to predict exactly which impacts which measures might have.

Transition management is the support of collective and cooperative attempts to advance sustainable social change within gradual and flexible processes; utilizing the interactive dynamics of socio-economic interdependencies, systematic innovation, and social visions. Transition management is a new approach to governance and social steering mechanisms that is neither traditional nor adheres strictly to the market-conformist mechanisms of increased economic efficiency. Recently implemented successfully in Dutch environmental and industrial programs, transition management has the integration of all levels of society as its goal and makes allowances for socio-cultural, economic, and institutional changes (see for example the work of the Dutch Research Institute for Transitions).

In this way, governance becomes an open process of learning and design reflected on all societal levels.

The term transition management is based on a multi-level governance model that furthers the implementation of sustainable development strategies on all important levels in concrete areas such as energy or transportation. Important elements of this model are:

- The use of strategic experiments
- The formulation of long-term goals and visions
- Iterative and interactive decision-making processes.

Transdisciplinary dialogue

The industrialized nations have a wealth of information at their fingertips, diverse technical possibilities, and enough financial means to overcome poverty, injustice, and environmental degradation. But they are apparently not (yet) able to transform this information and these means into constructive knowledge relevant for action. Why not? One reason is probably the social dialogue the relevant parties engage in. This dialogue should not be conducted only within specialized disciplines in their respective "ivory towers." A sustainable society needs a transdisciplinary dialogue.

Transdisciplinarity refers to the cooperation of academics and scientists across different disciplines together with non-academics involved in practical work. This includes political and economic decision-makers as well as concerned laypeople. Transdisciplinary cooperation is based on dialogue and cooperation;

the participants of such a dialogue should meet on an equal footing. This dialogue or cooperation has to be organized in a way that allows all participants the same opportunities to present their concerns.

Transdisciplinary processes are, however, often very difficult – due to widely divergent goals, methods, and values, or simply just different ways of speaking. For them to be successful, they need people who are able to initiate and support a critical dialogue. An active dialogue of all stakeholders and interested parties has many advantages for sustainable development as it ensures that, at least in the long term, a portion of the responsibility for the risks and opportunities of globalization and modernization is divided among many segments of society.

Sustainability science

The "Agenda 21," which emerged out of the Earth Summit in Rio de Janeiro (see Chapter 1), outlines the role of science and the importance of utilizing it for sustainable development. It also states that it is impossible to implement sustainable development without sustainability sciences.

Sustainability sciences can be characterized and differentiated from traditional sciences as follows:

–   The principles of sustainable development define new roles for sustainability scientists. Scientists become the initiators, facilitators, and coordinators of change, so to speak. They should act as facilitators of decision-making processes, as communicators, as teachers, students, and disseminators of knowledge. This kind of science must be very action-oriented.

–   Science and research oriented towards sustainable development must be an integral part of social development

processes. This requires that research goals are coherent
with sustainable development goals.
- Sustainability research is very complex and extensive, its
  results are therefore also broader than conventional research
  results (example of conventional research results are "new
  theories," data, models, information, and publications). In
  addition to these results, sustainability sciences also reach
  other, novel results meant to further the creation of human,
  social, and institutional capital.

Taken together, this adds up to new kinds of communication,
decision-making processes, and risk analyses; a new management of uncertainty factors; and a new quality control procedure
in developing decision-making processes.

Corporate citizenship

In recent years, the process of globalization and the concurrent liberalization of financial markets and trade have led to an
increase of economic (not necessarily business) activities. The
international linkage of financial markets has also increased the
number of concerned groups and people: governments, non-
governmental organizations, suppliers, participating citizens.
These are all so-called "stakeholders." In addition to economic
profit orientation, social and ecological criteria have also become
the focus of attention. Corporate citizenship describes businesses
as members of society who are to act responsibly towards other
members of society. Since all businesses can influence society on
the local and regional levels, they are able to use this influence
in a manner which allows both the local population and their
company to benefit. Successful corporate citizenship depends
upon whether a company has a coherent community involvement
strategy and realizes project partnerships; as well as whether its

efforts are broadly integrated into the company itself and its social commitment is meant to be long-term and sustainable. Corporate citizenship can therefore be seen as a contribution to sustainable development.

Corporate citizenship is closely connected to the idea of Corporate Social Responsibility, which refers to businesses' responsibility towards their employees and their families, to the local community, as well as to society as a whole. Environmental factors are also taken into account in this comprehensive concept, despite the focus on social needs. Community investment is one of the most visible forms of Corporate Social Responsibility.

Individual-level implementation

Traditional forms of membership in a religious congregation or in a political party, family and other values are currently increasingly being traded in for a pronounced individualism. This has many advantages, particularly more freedom of decision for a personal lifestyle. But it also has many disadvantages. The sociologist Lord Ralf Dahrendorf aptly calls this disorientation in a foundering world. The idea of sustainable development provides many proposals for transforming this disorientation into a new goal-oriented action, supporting both individualism and principles which create values. The concept of "quality of life" brings together normative standards of sustainable development and a joyous and peaceful search for orientation in a good and eminently livable world. Quality of life and sustainable development are thus very closely connected ideas.

According to a survey cited by Ernst Gehmacher – director of BOAS (*Büro für die Organisation angewandter Sozialforschung* – Office for the Organization of Applied Sociology) in Vienna who, as a scientist and Austrian OECD delegate in the project "Measuring Social Capital," triggered a broad public discourse on social capital and sustainable development – among sustainability experts, the number of those who themselves live in a sustainable manner is relatively low. Other studies have come up with results stating that 20 to 25% of the American and European population has beliefs, values, and lifestyles which hold the environment, relationships, peace, and justice higher than the mainstream population in these countries (see www.cultural-creatives.org). Their problem is that they know too little about one another and thus about their true social relevance. In fact, 20 to 25% of the population build a political, and also economic, factor that can no longer be ignored. As long as this continues to be widely disregarded by the mass media and is therefore also not present in the public consciousness, the Internet is perhaps a media suited to help people to communicate about individual (or common) concerns and thus to gain influence.

Sustainability scientists also know how difficult it is to implement sufficiency and sustainability on the individual level. Embedded in an utterly unsustainable environment, plagued by time constraints and professional obligations and the concurrent demands on mobility, they, too, travel by plane and car when running from meeting to meeting. However, in principle, each and every one of us can begin to help make sustainability become a reality for ourselves. And we can start today.

Suggestions for a sustainable lifestyle

The authors of this book would like to list some ways in which we can all contribute to a sustainable lifestyle in our industrialized world. This is in no way a complete list or "final" proposals.

We mostly want to show that it is really not so difficult to live more sustainably. All you need is a rudimentary knowledge of what you can do, an understanding of today's problems, and the desire to live sustainably. In this sense, the following suggestions should be understood as proposals for a dialogue with our readers which we would like to continue.

Food

Private consumer behavior is a key factor on the path towards sustainable development. Our eating habits provide an exemplary case for us to show how we can achieve a sustainable lifestyle.

Food scandals – from mad cow disease to vegetables contaminated with pesticides – have caused many people to question the way we feed ourselves. This has resulted in the increasing popularity of organic food. What we eat begins when we shop and ends with the disposal of the packaging and the leftovers. It is our decision whether we buy convenience food made of ingredients from far-away countries. When shopping, we can instead simply buy regional and organic products that have caused the least environmental impact both in production and in transportation, and whose production does not force other people into unacceptable working conditions. Everyone has the option of buying fair trade products – even if they cost somewhat more. These products guarantee that the producers enjoy a certain amount of social and health security and thus make a small contribution to the fight against poverty in developing countries.

The way we eat affects our environment, other people, and our health. It is easy to understand how the transportation of internationally traded foods and consumer goods have an environmental and social impact.

Water

The most important good in life is becoming scarce in many regions of the world. Already today, 1.2 billion people worldwide have no access to clean drinking water. The increase of pollutants in our environment is the main cause of unclean water. Even in areas rich in water, we need to conserve this vital resource. Water can be saved not only directly, but also indirectly. The resource savings due to decreasing meat consumption are enormous: According to Mauser, 35–70,000 liters of water are needed to produce one kilogram of imported beef. What we eat therefore directly affects water consumption in often far-away regions.

Mobility

In our globalized, fast-moving times, most of us are on the move quite a bit. But even if we are not mobile ourselves, we can take responsibility for whether or not the total amount of transportation increases by our consumer decisions (see above). Whether we go by bike, bus, or train, by car or by plane – our choice of means of transportation is decisive for protecting the climate and keeping the air clean (see Wagner). Of course walking, biking, and taking public transportation are the most environmentally-friendly means of transportation. Even for rest and recreation, an individually-owned car or a plane is never a sustainable means of transportation. Air traffic and individual motor traffic are the biggest "climate killers" – with all the known results.

Energy

Energy is currently the topic of the day. The information society, according to Wagner, has led to households and businesses owning a variety of household appliances, information devices, and office machines (audio and video players, televisions, cameras, telephones, computer accessories, and coffee makers).

For increased convenience, they are never completely turned off in a technical sense, but often run on standby. Chargers remain in outlets even when no phone is being charged. The standby consumption of each individual device is low. When, however, millions of devices are on standby, the total amount of electrical energy used is very high. Although this savings potential is not news, recent studies have shown that in Germany eighteen tera-watt hours (TWh), or 3% of total electricity production, are still used for standby functions. This amount is equivalent to half of all the electricity produced by all wind power plants in Germany in 2005, or to the electrical production of two atomic energy plants. Of course it is not possible to get rid of the losses caused by standby completely. A computer or printer cannot be turned off between jobs. However, televisions and audio equipment can be turned off completely at night, and we can unplug chargers that are not in use. Studies by the International Energy Agency show that up to 90% of standby electrical consumption in a household could be saved by a more conscious use of electricity.

Think globally – act locally

In our daily lives, we usually live together with people from dif-ferent backgrounds – whether at school, in our neighborhood, or at work. Living together enriches our lives, even when it some-times challenges our openness, tolerance, and understanding. It requires dialogue – communication between people. One indis-pensible precondition for leading a sustainable lifestyle is that we broaden our horizons, aware that Earth is a system, and that we are all a part of it, and that the actions of each and every one of us – whether they are sustainable or not – makes a difference.

Glossary

Ammonia: Ammonia emissions (NH3) are primarily
responsible for the creation of acidifying pollutants (and
also eutrophication). Agriculture is the main source of
ammonia emissions.

Biodiversity is the diversity of living organisms on Earth
and includes diversity within species (for example genetic
differences between individuals and populations) and
between species as well as the diversity of biological
communities and ecosystems.

Biosphere: Those parts of Earth and its atmosphere in which
life can occur. It encompasses living organisms (plants and
animals) and other organic material such as waste.

Carbon dioxide (CO_2) is a colorless, odorless gas that is a
natural element of the air in our atmosphere. CO_2 emissions
from burning fossil energy carriers (coal, crude oil, natural
gas) are the biggest cause of human-made climate change
today.

CFC: Abbreviation for chlorofluorocarbon. CFCs are largely
responsible for the depletion of the ozone layer since they
are dissociated by sunlight high in the atmosphere. They
then release chlorine compounds which attack and destroy
the ozone (the hole in the ozone layer).

Dematerialization refers to the production of goods and services in the future with a much lower input of material than is usual today.

Eco-efficiency: A certain output (production, in a broader sense also consumption) of goods and services is made with the lowest possible input of natural resources.

Ecological Footprint: The Ecological Footprint illustrates how much bioproductive land and water area is required for the long-term continuation of, for example, a city's or country's consumption of goods and services. It is calculated by determining both the use of natural resources and the absorption of greenhouse gas emissions.

Ecological rucksack: Ecological rucksacks allow visualizing the natural resources required along the whole production chain to produce a final product (or service). Every product (or service) has an ecological rucksack that consists of unused materials (e.g. mining waste), as well as all materials used in other countries to produce imported products.

Economic growth is the increase in the value of goods and services sold in one year by a country, region, or the whole world in comparison to the previous year.

Ecosphere is a synonym for biosphere (see *biosphere)*.

Ecosystem is a system of living creatures and their natural environment, including interdependencies. All of Earth's ecosystems taken together are called the biosphere or ecosphere.

Ecosystem services are those "services" which nature provides and human beings can use. Examples of ecosystem services are the pollination of fruit trees by insects, the provision of sweet water and drinking water by precipitation and natural filtration, the availability of fish for food in aquatic ecosystems, or the availability of fresh air.

Efficiency generally refers to achieving certain results with a lower input of work, resources, etc.

Environmental Space: The Environmental Space describes the total amount of energy, raw materials, and surface area that each person can utilize without causing irreversible damage to natural systems. The Environmental Space available per capita is equal for all people living on our planet.

Eutrophication denotes an increase in nutrients, usually in bodies of water. This increase changes the nutrient level of the water (from oligotrophic to mesotrophic to eutrophic and hypertrophic) and thus also the composition of the ecosystem.

Forest fragmentation: Splitting and dividing forests by streets and train tracks as well as by clearings for housing, industrial areas etc. Forest fragmentation leads to a separation effect; creating ecological barriers, isolation, and islands of wildlife habitats. The effect is particularly damaging when travel and breeding corridors are interrupted, preventing animal migration.

Globalization is the process of increasing international interdependencies of different regions of the world; particularly in the area of economic trade, but also in areas such as politics, culture, and the environment. Globalization is advanced particularly by progress in communication and transportation technologies, as well as by the liberalization of world trade.

Governance: In the broadest sense, governance is the mechanisms and rules by which socio-political systems (such as states, regions, or communities) are managed. Different mechanisms of coordination can be used. Currently, hierarchical steering mechanisms employed by the state (for example taxation) are, to some extent, becoming less important. Today, networks are also recognized as mechanisms of governance. In networks, (supra)national institutions attempt to cooperate with private sector organizations and civil society groups on a thematic, political level in order to guide individual policy areas. One role of the State in this case is to create a framework conducive to networking.

Happiness signifies a state of positive emotion which can be sustained over a long period of time. Human happiness can be measured in different ways. Accordingly, wealth and income are only one determinant of happiness. Above all, the quantity and quality of familial and social relationships play an important role, as do health, political environment (democracy), spiritual values, and the ability to reach goals one has set oneself. (See also *well-being*.)

Interdisciplinarity denotes cooperation on the part of people from different academic disciplines.

Invasive species are species that have spread to an area to which they are not indigenous without the direct or indirect influence of humans. Distinctions are made between non-native plants and non-native animals. These intruders can lead to problems, even causing native species to become extinct, by depriving them of nutrients or otherwise upsetting the balance of an ecosystem.

Isotopes of oxygen: An element, e.g. oxygen, is composed of one or a few stable isotopes distinguished by a varying number of neutrons in their nuclei. The most common stable isotope of oxygen is ^{16}O; ^{18}O also occurs naturally. Their proportion in ice cores can help estimate earlier average temperatures because water molecules containing the lighter ^{16}O evaporate faster. Layers of ice with a comparatively high percentage of ^{18}O therefore originate from warmer times.

Kyoto Protocol: The Kyoto Protocol was agreed upon in 1997
   by the 3rd Conference of the Parties of the UN Framework
   Convention on Climate Change. In the Protocol, the
   industrial countries commit to reducing their collective
   emissions of the most important greenhouse gases by at
   least 5% below 1990 levels between 2008 and 2012. To reach
   this goal, countries have committed to different emission
   reduction obligations.

Material intensity describes the amount of (raw) materials
   necessary to make one unit of economic value added. It
   is calculated in metric tons per euro (see also *resource
   productivity*).

Mixed work is a term referring to all types of work. It includes
   paid labor (employed or freelance, full-time or part-time)
   as well as unpaid labor for oneself (for example cooking for
   oneself, learning), reproductive work (raising children, care
   of relatives) and community work (voluntary activities).

Natural capital: All areas of nature and ecosystems which
   provide goods and services to mankind (see also *natural
   resources* and *ecosystem services*).

Natural resources are all raw materials needed by humans
   to produce goods and provide services. A distinction is
   made between renewable (for example food, wood) and
   non-renewable (for example fossil energy carriers, metals)
   resources.

Nitrogen oxides (NO_x) include nitrogen monoxide (NO) and
   nitrogen dioxide (N_2O). N_2O is particularly harmful to
   humans, damaging the function of the lungs. Together with
   hydrocarbons, nitric oxides lead to the creation of ozone
   in the summer. Furthermore, nitric oxides are partially
   responsible for the eutrophication (overfertilization) of soils
   and bodies of water. In the cold seasons, gaseous nitric

oxides and ammonia create particular ammonium nitrate, which contributes to the large-scale distribution of fine particulate matter (PM10).

Non-methane volatile organic compounds (NMVOC) are emitted primarily by the evaporation of solvents and fuels as well as by incomplete combustion. Biogenic sources, particularly forests, also make a non-negligible contribution. These compounds are important above all because of their contribution to the formation of ozone in the troposphere (the atmospheric layer nearest the Earth).

Organic solvents are liquid at room temperature and evaporate more or less easily. They are volatile substances which can easily be mixed with other substances without chemically changing themselves or the other materials. Organic solvents can be found in varnishes, paints, glues, wood preservatives, stains, etc. These compounds are precursors for the creation of ozone in the lower atmosphere.

Permafrost is soil below a certain depth which is frozen throughout the year. It may thaw on the surface in the summer. Large parts of northern Canada, Alaska, Greenland, and eastern Siberia consist of permafrost. The depth of permafrost differs. In northern Russia, permafrost can reach depths of 1450 meters (4757.2 feet); in Scandinavia the permafrost depth is only 20 meters (65.6 feet).

Pesticides: Umbrella term for all chemical pest control substances. The most common pesticides are insecticides, herbicides, and fungicides. Many pesticides have unwanted side effects. In the past, they made their way into the food chain causing damage to humans and animals. Legal measures have greatly reduced pesticide residues in the food chain today.

pH is a measure of the acidity or alkalinity of a solution. A pH value of less than seven indicates an acidic solution, neutral solutions have a pH of seven, and pH greater than seven indicates an alkaline solution.

Phytoplankton are plant plankton (diatoms, blue-green algae, golden algae, etc.). They are found in standing and slow-moving waters where they are at the bottom of the food pyramid. They are eaten by zooplankton and animals that live on the ocean floor and at the bottom of inland waters. They obtain energy by the photosynthesis of CO_2 and nutrients.

Plant genetic engineering is the practical application of molecular biology research and methods. Plant genetic engineering is based on the fact that samples of tissue or even single cells of a plant can "regenerate" and develop into a complete organism. Using plant genetic engineering, genes or combinations of genes can be inserted into plants despite reproductive barriers. Use of suitable steering elements enables programming of the parameter value of genetically modified properties to ensure that the new plant exhibits certain characteristics.

Polluter pays principle: The polluter pays principle is the maxim pertaining to all areas of the environment, applicable to both producers and consumers, which states that whoever causes environmental impact must carry the costs of their actions or failure to act.

ppm (parts per million) is a numerical value given in millionths, just as percent (%) is a value given in hundredths.

Precautionary principle: The precautionary principle is an important doctrine of current environmental policy which requires avoiding risks and dangers to the environment before they occur, or keeping them at an absolute minimum.

It thus makes provisions for risks and dangers. At the Earth Summit it was explained as follows: "In the face of threats of irreversible environmental damage, lack of full scientific understanding should not be an excuse for postponing actions which are justified in their own right. The precautionary approach could provide a basis for policies relating to complex systems that are not yet fully understood and whose consequences of disturbances cannot yet be predicted."

Prognosis: The prediction of an event, condition or development.

Prosperity is an umbrella term for all objective factors which determine the quality of life of a person or an entire population.

Resource productivity is defined as the amount of economic value added (e.g. euros) that can be gained from one unit of natural resources (e.g. one metric ton of aluminum). Resource productivity is inverse to material intensity.

Scenarios are descriptions of possible paths we can take into the future. They are based on assumptions about the development of current trends, possibilities of resolving critical uncertainties, and which new factors will become influential. Scenarios are neither forecasts nor prognoses. They are images of possible paths to, and conditions in, the future that show us what could happen given different assumptions.

Social capital refers to the relationships between people and organizations necessary for the functioning of societies based on the division of labor. OECD measurements of social capital show a quantitative and qualitative decline of these relationships.

Social metabolism is the exchange of material and energy between a societal system (a city or a country) and nature (see also *eco-efficiency*).

Subsidiarity is the principle that decisions should, whenever possible, be made at the lowest level of the social hierarchy (community, region, city), and higher levels (national governments, EU, UN) should intervene only when overriding interests are at stake.

Sufficiency refers to being content with an adequate amount of material things. Adequate in turn can be defined as everything which is not too much. If we agree that from a certain level of material prosperity on, it is no longer possible to greatly increase individual happiness or well-being, then the industrialized countries have substantial potential to increase both sufficiency and the quality of life.

Sulfur dioxide (SO_2) is generated above all by the combustion of coal and heavy fuel oils. In high concentrations, SO_2 damages humans, animals, and plants; the products of its oxidation cause "acid rain." Acid rain endangers sensitive ecosystems such as forests and lakes; it also causes damage to buildings and materials. Sulfate particles contribute to the large-scale distribution of fine particulate matter.

Sustainable development is development which ensures that economic performance and social security are in harmony with the long-term preservation of natural resources.

System: A system consists of a (larger) number of elements and their characteristics as well as the relationships between these elements and between them and their surrounding environment.

Temperature of the Earth: The average temperature of the Earth is used as an indicator for global warming due to climate change. It is the result of the balance of thermal

energy received from the sun (short wave spectrum) and
thermal energy radiated by the Earth (long wave spectrum).

Threshold: A threshold is the lowest physical or physiological
point sufficient to cause a verifiable change.

Transdisciplinary: Transdisciplinarity refers to the cooperation
of academics and scientists across different disciplines
together with non-academics involved in practical work in
order to solve problems.

Transition management is the collective and cooperative
attempt to advance sustainable societal change step by step
with the participation of as many societal actors as possible
(governance). This form of management attempts to take
the iterative dynamic of socio-economic interdependencies
into account.

Well-being is the subjective feeling of contentedness with one's
individual quality of life.

Work-life balance is a life in which paid labor, recreation,
community work, and reproductive work are in equilibrium.

References

I Global change

Carson, Rachel. 1962. *Silent Spring.* New York: Houghton Mifflin Company.

Crutzen, Paul. 1997. "Das stratosphärische Ozonloch: Eine durch menschliche Aktivitäten erzeugte chemische Instabilität in der Atmosphäre," in Bundesministerium für Umwelt, Naturzschutz und Reaktorsicherheit, ed., 10 *Jahre Montrealer Protokoll.* Bonn: Reihe Umweltpolitik.

Fischer, Ernst Peter and Klaus Wiegandt, eds. 2005. *Die Zukunft der Erde. Was verträgt unser Planet noch?* Frankfurt a. M.: S. Fischer Verlag.

Luhmann, Hans-Jochen. 2001. *Die Blindheit der Gesellschaft.* Munich: Gerling Akademie Verlag.

Mauser, Wolfram. "Das blaue Gold," in Fischer, Ernst Peter and Klaus Wiegandt, eds. 2005. *Die Zukunft der Erde. Was verträgt unser Planet noch?* Frankfurt a. M.: S. Fischer Verlag.

Meadows, Dennis, et al. 1972. *The Limits to Growth. A Report for the Club of Rome's Project on the Predicament of Mankind.* New York: Universe Books.

Münz, Rainer. "Weltbevölkerung und weltweite Migration. Wie weit wächst die Zahl der Menschen?" in Fischer, Ernst Peter and Klaus Wiegandt, eds. 2005. *Die Zukunft der Erde. Was verträgt unser Planet noch?* Frankfurt a. M.: S. Fischer Verlag.

Richardson, Katherine. "Der globale Wandel und die Zukunft der Ozeane. Auf dem Weg zu einer Wissenschaft für das System Erde," in Fischer, Ernst Peter and Klaus Wiegandt, eds. 2005. *Die Zukunft der Erde. Was verträgt unser Planet noch?* Frankfurt a. M.: S. Fischer Verlag.

Steffen, Will, et al. 2004. *Global Change and the Earth System. A Planet under Pressure.* Berlin: Springer.

UNDP, et al. 2005. *The Wealth of the Poor: Managing Ecosystems to Fight Poverty.* Washington, D. C.: World Resources Institute.

World Commission on Environment and Development. 1987. *Our Common Future.* Oxford: Oxford Paperbacks.

Wuppertal Institute. 2005. *Fair Future – Begrenzte Ressourcen und Globale Gerechtigkeit.* Wuppertal: Beck.

For further information on topics covered in this chapter:

Earth Portal: http://www.earthportal.org/

Forum on Science and Innovation for Sustainable Development: http://sustainabilityscience.org

German Advisory Council on Global Change: http://www.wbgu.de/wbgu_home_engl.html

Sustainable Europe Research Institute: http://www.seri.at

UK Sustainable Development Commission: http://www.sd-commission.org.uk/

UN Commission on Sustainable Development: http://www.un.org/esa/sustdev/csd/review.htm

2 The Earth System

Flannery, Tim. 2005. *The Weather Makers*. London: Penguin Books.

Fuggle, R. F. "Lake Victoria: A case study of complex interrelationships," in UNEP. 2004. *Africa Environmental Outlook. Case Studies. Human Vulnerability to Environmental Change*. Nairobi: UNEP: 75–85.

Gordon, Chris and Julius K. Ametekpor, eds. 1999. *The sustainable integrated development of the Volta Basin in Ghana*. Accra: Volta Basin Research Project.

Harremoës, Poul, David Gee, and Malcolm MacGarvin, eds. 2002. *Late lessons from early warnings: the precautionary principle 1896–2002*. Brussels: European Environment Agency. http://reports.eea.europa.eu/environmental_issue_report_2001_22/en.

Houghton, J.T., ed. 2001. *Climate Change 2001: The Scientific Basis:* Contribution of Working Group I to the Third Assessment Report of the Intergovernmental Panel on Climate Change. Cambridge: Cambridge University Press.

Keeling, C. D. and T. P. Whorf. 2000. "Atmospheric CO_2 records from sites in the SIO air sampling network," in US Department of Energy (ed.). *Trends: A compendium of data on global change*. Oak Ridge, TN: Carbon Dioxide Information Analysis Center, Oak Ridge National Laboratory, US Department of Energy.

Kromp-Kolb, Helga and Herbert Formayer. 2005. *Schwarzbuch Klimawandel. Wie viel Zeit bleibt uns noch?* Salzburg: Ecowin Verlag.

Latif, Mojib. 2008. *Climate Change: The Point of No Return*. London: Haus Publishing (in press).

Petit, J. R., et al. 1999. "Climate and atmospheric history of the past 420,000 years from the Vostok ice core, Antarctica," in *Nature* 399: 429–436.

Richardson, Katherine. "Der globale Wandel und die Zukunft der Ozeane. Auf dem Weg zu einer Wissenschaft für das System Erde," in Fischer, Ernst Peter and Klaus Wiegandt, eds. 2005. *Die Zukunft der Erde. Was verträgt unser Planet noch?* Frankfurt a. M.: S. Fischer Verlag.

Steffen, Will, et al. 2004. *Global Change and the Earth System: A Planet Under Pressure.* Berlin: Springer.

UNEP, United Nations Environment Programme. 1999. *Global Environmental Outlook 2000.* http://www.unep.org/geo.

UNEP, United Nations Environment Programme. 2002. *Global Environmental Outlook 3.* http://www.unep.org/geo.

Wagner, Hermann-Josef. 2008. *Energy: The World's Race for Resources in the 21st Century.* London: Haus Publishing (in press).

For further information on topics covered in this chapter:
Earth System Science Partnership: http://www.essp.org/
European Environment Agency: http://www.eea.europa.eu/
Intergovernmental Panel on Climate Change:
      http://www.ipcc.org
International Institute for Sustainable Development:
      http://www.iisd.org/

3 Resource Use – We're Living Beyond Our Means

Behrens, A., Giljum, S., Kovanda, J., Niza, S. 2007. "The material basis of the global economy. World-wide patterns in natural resource extraction and their implications for sustainable resource use policies." *Ecological Economics* 64, 444–453.

Binswanger, H. C.: 2006. *Die Wachstumsspirale. Geld, Energie und Imagination in der Dynamik des Marktprozesses.* Marburg: Metropolis.

Daly, Herman E. 1996. *Beyond Growth.* Boston, MA: Beacon Press.

Diamond, Jared. 1995. "Easter Island's End," in *Discover* 1995: 63–69.

The Economist. 2008. "A ravenous dragon. China's quest for resources." *Economist* Special Report, London.

Fischer-Kowalski, M. 1998. "Society´s Metabolism." In: Redclift, G., Woodgate, G. (Eds.), *International Handbook of Environmental Sociology.* Edward Elgar, Cheltenham.

Hahlbrock, Klaus. 2008. *Feeding the Planet: Environmental Protection through Sustainable Agriculture.* London: Haus Publishing (in press).

International Energy Agency (IEA). 2004. *CO_2 Emissions from Fossil Fuel Combustion.* Paris. Electronic database available online at: http://data.iea.org/ieastore/default.asp.

Jancke, G. 1999. *Ansatz zur Berechnung und Vermittlung der Nachhaltigkeit der Stadt Hamburg mit Hilfe eines aggregierten Indikators-Möglichkeiten der Nutzung im lokalen Agenda 21-Prozeß.* Lüneburg: University of Lüneburg, Institute for Environmental Communication.

Latif, Mojib. 2008. *Climate Change: The Point of No Return.* London: Haus Publishing (in press).

Meadows, Dennis, et al. 1972. *The Limits to Growth: A Report for the Club of Rome's Project on the Predicament of Mankind.* New York: Universe Books.

Myers, N., J. Kent. 2003. "New consumers. The influence of affluence on the environment," in *PNAS* 100 (8): 4963–4968.

Neumayer, Eric. 2003. *Weak Versus Strong Sustainability: Exploring the Limits of Two Opposing Paradigms.* Cheltenham: Edward Elgar Publishing.

Opschoor, J. B. 1995. "Ecospace and the fall and rise of throughput intensity," in *Ecological Economics* 15: 137–141.

Porritt, Jonathon. 2005. *Capitalism as if the world matters.* London: Earthscan.

Riedl, Rupert and Manuela Delpos, eds. 1996. *Die Ursachen des Wachstums. Unsere Chancen zur Umkehr.* Vienna: Kremayr & Scheriau.

Schmidt-Bleek, Friedrich, ed. 2004. *Der ökologische Rucksack. Wirtschaft für eine Zukunft mit Zukunft.* Stuttgart: Hirzel.

Schmidt-Bleek, Friedrich. 2008. *The Earth: Natural Resources and Human Intervention.* London: Haus Publishing (in press).

Schnauss, M. 2001. *Der ökologische Fußabdruck der Stadt Berlin.* Berlin: Berlin House of Representatives Enquete Commission "Lokale Agenda 21 / Zukunftsfähiges Berlin."

Schütz, H., Bringezu, S., Moll, S. 2004. *Globalisation and the shifting environmental burden. Material trade flows of the European Union.* Wuppertal Institute, Wuppertal.

Sieferle, R. P. 2001. *The Subterranean Forest: Energy Systems and the Industrial Revolution.* The White Horse Press, Isle of Harris, UK.

Spangenberg, J., ed. 1995. *Towards Sustainable Europe. The study.* London: Friends of the Earth.

Wackernagel, M., Rees, W. 1996. *Our Ecological Footprint: Reducing Human Impact on the Earth.* New Society Publishers, Gabriola Island, British Columbia.

World Bank. 2003. *Global economic prospects: Realizing the developing promise of the Doha agenda.* Washington: World Bank.

World Resources Institute. 2005. *Earth Trends. Environmental Information*. Washington: http://earthtrends.wri.org.

World Trade Organization. 2005. *International trade statistics*. Geneva: WTO.

Wuppertal Institute. 2005. *Fair Future – Begrenzte Ressourcen und Globale Gerechtigkeit*. Wuppertal: Beck.

WWF, Zoological Society of London, Global Footprint Network. 2006. *Living Planet Report 2006*. WWF, Gland, Switzerland.

For further information on topics covered in this chapter:

Global Footprint Network: http://www.footprintnetwork.org

Online portal for material flow data:
http://www.materialflows.net

Sustainable Europe Research Institute: http://www.seri.at

Wuppertal Institute for Climate, Environment and Energy:
http://www.wupperinst.org/en/home/index.html

4 Visions of a Sustainable Future

Aachener Stiftung Kathy Beys, ed. 2005. *Ressourcenproduktivität als Chance-Ein langfristiges Konjunkturprogramm für Deutschland*. Norderstedt: Books on Demand.

Bergmann, Frithjof. 2005. *Neue Arbeit, neue Kultur*. Freiamt: Arbor.

BMFSFJ (German Federal Ministry of Family Affairs, Senior Citizens, Women and Youth) and German Federal Statistical Office. 2003. Wo *bleibt die Zeit? Die Zeitverwendung der Bevölkerung in Deutschland 2001/2002*. http://www.destatis.de/presse/deutsch/pk/2003/wbdz.pdf.

Brandl, Sebastian and Eckart Hildebrandt. 2002. *Zukunft der Arbeit und soziale Nachhaltigkeit*. Opladen: Leske und Budrich. Reihe Soziologie und Ökologie, Band 8.

Fischer, H., et al. 2004. "Wachstums- und Beschäftigungsimpulse rentabler Materialeinsparungen," in *Wirtschaftsdienst* 2004/04.

Frey, Bruno and Alois Stutzer. 2005. "Happiness Research: State and Prospects," in *Review of Social Economy*. 62(2):207–228.

Gehmacher, Ernst, Sigrid Kroismayr and Josef Neumüller. 2006. *Sozialkapital. Neue Zugänge zu gesellschaftlichen Kräften*. Vienna: Mandelbaum Verlag.

Grimm, Jordis. 2006. *Glücksforschung-und was Regionen davon lernen können. SERI Background Paper No. 10* Vienna: www.sert.at.

Jasch, Ch. and D. Savage. 2005. *International Guidance Document: Environmental Management Accounting*. International Federation of Accountants New York: IFAC, http://www.ifac.org/Store/Details. tmpl?SID=11235959393318284.

Kahnemann, Daniel and Alan Krueger. 2006. "Developments in the Measurement of Subjective Well-Being," in *Journal of Economic Perspectives*, 20(1):3–24.

Layard, Richard. 2005. *Happiness: Lessons from a New Science*. New York: Penguin Press HC.

NEF, New Economics Foundation. 2004. "A Well-Being Manifesto for a Flourishing Society," in *The Power of Well-Being* Paper No 3.

Putnam, R. D. 2000: *Bowling Alone*. New York: Simon and Schuster Paperbacks.

Schaffer, Axel and Carsten Stahmer. 2005. "*Die Halbtagsgesellschaft-ein Konzept für nachhaltigere*

Produktions- und Konsummuster," in *GAIA – Ecological Perspectives for Science and Society* 3/2005: 229–239.

Stocker, Andrea, Friedrich Hinterberger and Sophie Strasser. "Verteilung von Arbeit und Einkommen," in Susanne Hartard, Carsten Stahmer und Axel Schaffer, eds. 2006. *Die Halbtagsgesellschaft-konkrete Utopie für eine zukunftsfähige Gesellschaft.* Baden-Baden: Nomos Verlag.

Weizsäcker, Ernst Ulrich von, Amory Lovins and L. Hunter Lovins. 1998. *Factor Four: Doubling Wealth, Halving Resource Use – A Report to the Club of Rome.* London: Earthscan Ltd.

For further information on topics covered in this chapter:
New Economics Foundation:
  http://www.neweconomics.org/gen
UK Sustainable Development Commission:
  http://www.sd-commission.org.uk
World Database of Happiness:
  http://worlddatabaseofhappiness.eur.nl

5 Paths towards Sustainability

Commission of the European Communities. 2001. *European Governance. A white Paper.* COM (2001) 428.

Dahrendorf, Ralf. 2005. *Auf der Suche nach einer neuen Ordnung.* München: C.H.Beck.

Fischer, Ernst Peter and Klaus Wiegandt, eds. 2005. *Die Zukunft der Erde. Was verträgt unser Planet noch?* Frankfurt a. M.: S. Fischer Verlag.

Forum Sustainable Austria, ed. 2006. *Trend Study on Unsustainability*. http://www.nachhaltigkeit.at/strategie. php3?forum=aktivitaeten.

Hüther, Michael. 1990. *Integrierte Steuer-Transfer-Systeme für die Bundesrepublik Deutschland: normative Konzeption und empirische Analyse*. Berlin: Duncker & Humblot GmbH.

International Energy Agency. 2005. *Fact Sheet: Standby Power Use and IEA "1-Watt Plan."* http://www.iea.org/Textbase/ publications/free_new_Desc.asp?PUBS_ID=1553

Kraus, D., et al. 2006. "Leerlaufverbrauch strombetriebener Haushalts- und Bürogeräte," in *Energiewirtschaftliche Tagesfragen*, 56(4): 60–63 (part 1) and (5): 44–48 (part 2).

Mauser, Wolfram. "Das blaue Gold: Wasser," in Fischer, Ernst Peter and Klaus Wiegandt, eds. 2005. *Die Zukunft der Erde. Was verträgt unser Planet noch?* Frankfurt a. M.: S. Fischer Verlag.

Voss, Jan-Peter, Dierk Bauknecht, and René Kemp, eds. 2006. *Reflexive Governance for Sustainable Development*. Cheltenham: Edward Elgar Publishing.

Wagner, Hermann-Josef. 2008. *Energy: The World's Race for Resources in the 21st Century*. London: Haus Publishing (in press).

Watkins, Kevin and Penny Fowler. 2002. *Rigged rules and double standards. Trade, globalisation and the fight against poverty*. Oxford, UK: Oxfam Campaign Reports.

For further information on topics covered in this chapter:
Attac: http://www.attac.org/?lang=en
Dutch Research Institute for Transitions:
http://www.drift.eur.nl
Global Marshall Plan: http://www.globalmarshallplan.org/ index_eng.html

Report from the Commission on European Governance: http://
    ec.europa.eu/governance/docs/comm_rapport_en.pdf
URGENDA – A Dutch Garden of Sustainability Experiments:
    http://www.urgenda.nl/?page=signup_en

Illustrations

Fig. 1.1, 1.3, 2.3 adapted from Steffen et al. 2004; Fig.1.4
adapted from Schellnhuber, 2000; Fig. 2.2 adapted from Petit et
al. 1999; Fig. 2.4, 2.5 adapted from Kromp-Kolb and Formayer,
2005; Fig. 3.1 adapted from Bringezu, 2000; Fig. 3.2 adapted
from Daly, 1999; Fig. 3.3 adapted from International Energy
Agency (IEA) figure, 2004; Fig. 3.4 adapted from Wuppertal
Institute 2005; Fig. 4.1 adapted from Hannover Chamber of
Commerce; Fig. 4.2 adapted from NEF, 2004; All figures: Peter
Palm, Berlin.